SPENNYMOOR REMEMBERED - BOOK 3

SPENNYMOOR REMEMBERED
BOOK - 3

SPENNYMOOR REMEMBERED - BOOK 3

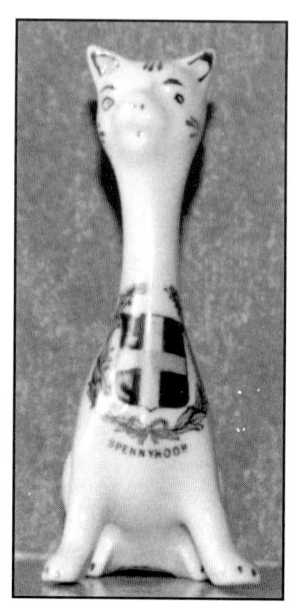

SPENNYMOOR COMMEMERATIVE WARE

SPENNYMOOR REMEMBERED
BOOK - 3

Compiled by
Bob Abley

ARB PUBLICATIONS

SPENNYMOOR REMEMBERED - BOOK 3

First Published 2001
Copyright c. Bob Abley, 2001

Published by
ARB Publications
98 Durham Road
Spennymoor
County Durham
DL16 6SQ

ISBN 09536315 2 4

Printed in Great Britain by
Macdonald Press
Spennymoor
County Durham

SPENNYMOOR REMEMBERED - BOOK 3

Contents

Acknowledgements		6
Introduction		7
1.	In and Around the Town	9
2.	Schools	23
3.	Byers Green	39
4	People and Events	59
5	Trade Transport and Industry	103

SPENNYMOOR REMEMBERED - BOOK 3

Acknowledgements.

Once again I am indebted to many people for help given in the compilation of this book. I am extremely grateful for the time, information and material freely and generously given. I would particularly like to thank the following people without whose help and encouragement the book could not have been completed: Bill Kitching, Brenda Dunn, Alf Todd, Frank Tressiter, Mrs. Ellerby, Mrs. Mutton, Allan Spencer, Ray Johnson, Bob Richmond, Michael Bostock (senior), Michael Bostock (junior), Jack Murray, Mr. and Mrs. Gilbert Anderson, Harry Spence, Phil Rhymer, Neil Kelly, Mr. and Mrs. Hodges, Enid Barr, Vera Brydon, Sylvia Foster, Bill and Enid Scorer, Jim Henderson, Sandra Clayton, Marjorie Connor, John Asquith, Mr. Vincent, Mr. and Mrs. Bell Mrs. Waggot, Tom Hutchinson and Harry and Barbara Lennon.

SPENNYMOOR REMEMBERED - BOOK 3

Introduction

The format of the book is the same as in previous years and again the compiling of the book has proved both enjoyable and interesting. I have been most fortunate in being able to meet and talk to Alf Todd of Byers Green who at the age of 92 is a veritable fount of knowledge on the history of the area. By happy coincidence I have also been able to make use of a good collection of Byers Green photographs for which Alf has provided much interesting detail. I have also been fortunate in having access to the notes on aspects of local history compiled by Frank Tressiter and have found them particulary valuable in relation to local mining history.

I would like to broaden the appeal in future books by including detailed sections on Croxdale, Page Bank, Kirk Merrington, Leasingthorne, Middlestone, Westerton, and perhaps Hett so if anyone has any photographs or reminiscences they would like to share I would be pleased to hear from them.

In the new year, 2002, I hope to have a web site up and running to provide for news, views and discussion on all aspects of local history relevant to the local area. So watch out for www.spennymoorremembered.co.uk in January 2002. As another new departure I am making available to Durham County Library Service a number of photographs which have been used in the Spennymoor Remembered Series, these will be able to be accessed on computer at the Spennymoor Branch Library. It is hoped that these will be useful to people doing research of their own, for students or just for general interest.

SPENNYMOOR REMEMBERED - BOOK 3

Cambridge Corner
for SWEETS

TOBACCO and CIGARETTES

Mr H. B. Dees,
19, Weardale St.,
Spennymoor.

Painter and Decorator.

Specialist in Modern Decoration.

TO LOOK WELL
You must look well dressed

LOOK IN AT

Madame Meredith's

and you will always

LOOK YOUR BEST

Phone 3153

WHITWORTH COMMERCIAL SCHOOL.

Mr & Mrs W. Christison,
45, Whitworth Terrace,
Spennymoor.

Day and Evening Commercial Classes.

Shorthand, Typewriting, Book Keeping.

Typewriting and Duplicating.

WORK PROMPTLY CARRIED OUT.

W. H. SNOWDON
CHEMIST

National Health Dispensing

46, High St.
Spennymoor.

SPENNYMOOR REMEMBERED – BOOK 3

ONE

IN AND AROUND TOWN

Looking up through the Bridge 1967.
French's tobacconist shop on the left with the gleaming Mercedes parked outside, perhaps that was the object of taking the photograph rather than the general view.

The Travellers Rest Thomas Street 1976.

Back Thomas Street
This was the scene prior to demolition in 1976

SPENNYMOOR REMEMBERED – BOOK 3

Miners Banner being paraded along King Street c.1912
It seems that the parade has been held to celebrate the opening of the aged miner's homes. The second, smaller banner reads "Success To The Aged Miners Homes." The earliest aged miner's homes to be built in the Spennymoor area were built at Middlestone Moor.

Page Bank Long Row 1930.
Page Bank a colliery village built with the opening of Page Bank Colliery in 1853, it outlasted the Pit, which closed in 1936 but succumbed to the floods during the 1960's. A whole community gone but not forgotten, yet!

The Red Lion 1959.
The Red Lion was in Queen Street, the start of Ox Close Crescent can be seen in the background.

Tudhoe Lane 1910.

Whitworth Hall Gardens c.1920

Masons Arms 1962.
The buildings in the centre foreground were once the original Middlestone Moor Working Men's Club. In the top left corner you can see part of the old chapel that was converted into a pram factory. The allotments behind Oak Dean Terrace have now been built on.

SPENNYMOOR REMEMBERED – BOOK 3

The Top House, Middlestone Moor 1962.
The pub was always known as the Top House, being the last pub in Middlestone Moor, its proper name being the Excelsior. The Binchester Hotel was the Bottom House and the Masons' Arms the Middle House. This site was finally demolished during the early 1990's and redeveped with new housing. To the right are the premises of Dunelm Granite, the monumental stonemasons. Behind the pub itself are the remnants of Nutters Buildings, which provided accommodation for the miners of Binchester Colliery. The Duke of Windsor famously visited Nutters Buildings during the depression. The road running at an angle to Dunelm Granite was the pit road leading to Binchester Colliery.

Tudhoe Woods 1910.

SPENNYMOOR REMEMBERED – BOOK 3

Mid Clyde Terrace 1962.

The large house, front centre, was originally Clyde House and was later split into two, one part being Clyde House and the other Lothian House. Part of the premises was used for a long time as a dentist surgery first by Mr. Lawrence and then by Geoff Carr. The orchard at the back of the house was sold off during the late 1960's and provided the site for the present bungalows. The rest of the site was eventually levelled during the early 1990's and redeveloped as a nursing home retaining the name Lothian House. To the right is the Hillingdon pub, this building did not start out as a pub it was a private residence, called Hillingdon House, belonging to Rowland Hill who had a chemist shop in Spennymoor. It was converted into a pub during the 1930's. The house behind and to the right of the Hillingdon is Hawthorn House. Top left is the remnants of the racecourse the section of it in view being used by the owners, Teasdales, as a battery hen farm.

The housing estate was the first council housing estate to be built in Spennymoor, it was built just before the beginning of the Second World War and was a model estate, with wide roads semi - detached houses and spacious gardens. Some of the houses had five bedrooms to accommodate the larger families of those days.

The shop at the front left was Stearman's with a long established grocery and off-license business; they had another shop in Middlestone Moor.

SPENNYMOOR REMEMBERED – BOOK 3

St. Andrew's Church 1962.

Work was just being completed on levelling the old iron works site off prior to building the new road system and Bessemer Park Housing Estate. The dogleg in the original road can be clearly seen, the car, on the road, has just come down Dobbie's Bank to go through the dogleg into Barnfield Road. Dobbie's Bank, leading down from Mount Pleasant, was so named because Andrew Hall's Shop at the top off the bank was managed by Sid Dobson. Previous to this it had been know as Skipsy's Bank because the owner of the shop was called Skipsy.

In the left foreground is the site of the old gasworks, all that remains are semi-detached houses, which had once been the manager's house and the gasworks office.

The vicarage has not yet been built on the site next to the church, at this time it was situated in North Road. Built on the church land is Siemens Social Club, This club was built for the factory workers and in its heyday, during the late fifties and early sixties, was a well known and well supported place for entertainment. The site of this club is now taken up by the Parish hall.

To the right of the church the new housing estate in St. Andrew's Road it just nearing completion. The early sixties marked the beginning of big changes in the town, not least in this area.

SPENNYMOOR REMEMBERED – BOOK 3

Tudhoe Colliery c.1924.

Tudhoe Colliery Housing.

When the Pit opened in 1866, the influx of miners and workers created a great demand for houses. Miners and their families came to the area from as far as Cornwall and Wales. Houses were quickly but solidly built of stone to accommodate them, the stone being quarried at York Hill. Over 300 houses were built in three rows. The row built on the main road was called Front Street and had 124 houses divided into blocks. On each end of the blocks larger houses were erected by extending into the yard, these houses were for officials in the pit. The other two rows of houses were built nearer the pit, behind, Front Street, these were Middle row and Back Row.

Front Street had back yards and gardens at the front, they were four roomed houses, two up and two down. The Middle row also had four rooms but an open yard and no garden. Back Row had three roomed houses with no garden and no separate yard. There was a bricked footpath at the rear which ran the whole length of the row and it was kept scrubbed clean by the householders. These houses had a lean-to pantry cum back kitchen.

The size of the miner's family determined what size house you were allotted. Newlyweds or families with no children were given Back Row houses and moved to a bigger house when their family increased.

Mr. Dakers who was one time colliery manager used to walk from his house, The Loggins, to the Colliery Offices which were at 49 and 50 Front Street and inspect the gardens. Any miner with a garden that was not cultivated to Mr. Dakers satisfaction was immediately banished with his family to one of the back rows.

The block of houses nearest Tudhoe Colliery School was named locally School Row and most of these houses were occupied by officials in the pit, overmen, chargehands, engineers and electricians etc. One of the houses was used as a reading room and was in great use during the 1921 and 1926 strikes. They were also used as committee rooms for the labour party during elections.

From the notes of the late W.G.Mutton.

SPENNYMOOR REMEMBERED – BOOK 3

Tudhoe Colliery Middle Row c.1900

Cottages at the bottom end of Tudhoe Village

SPENNYMOOR REMEMBERED – BOOK 3

Demolition of King James Street 1970
Winnie Johnson's shop is on the corner.

The newly designated main road, Oxford Street.
The wagons are queuing to remove the rubble that was once King William Street. The clearance of the houses on the right was originally earmarked as the site of the new bus station but the plan was changed to accommodate the new Co-op Superstore.

SPENNYMOOR REMEMBERED – BOOK 3

Mr. Jack Rhymer.
An ex. resident of King James Street contemplates the destruction that is going on around him.

King William Street prior to demolition.
The flats of Bessmer Park looming in the background, progress indeed!

SPENNYMOOR REMEMBERED – BOOK 3

King John Street 1918.
Decorated to celebrate the end of the First World War.

Site of Hartley Terrace c.1963,
Durham Road in the background with the rear of Hardy's off-license shop in the centre. Most of Hartley Terrace and the lower part of South terrace had been demolished to make way for the building of the old folk's home complex, which exists today.

SPENNYMOOR REMEMBERED – BOOK 3

Rock Road 1963. The cemetery on the right and the wall of the recently built Spennymoor West Modern School on the left. There were particularly heavy snowfalls during the winter of 1963, this one providing us with the perfect peaceful wintry scene.

Cheapside during the early 1940's

SPENNYMOOR REMEMBERED - BOOK 3

TWO

SCHOOLS

Alderman Wraith 1948.
Front Row: Arnold Roberts, Eric Pattison, Derek Leathley,, Billy Troupe, David Williams, Peter Mathews, Derek Bracey, Colin Scott, Hasrry Eltringham and Eric Simpson
Middle Row: June Barron, Lillian Moody, Sybill Black, Jean Lavell, Eva Ward, Miss Watchman, Peggy Harrison, Valerie Ward, Sheila Wigham, Ellen Kenan and Norma Nicholson.
Front Row. Joan Richardson, Zillah Patterson, Betty Brough, Pat Cockayne, Betty Harman and Edith Robinson.

SPENNYMOOR REMEMBERED - BOOK 3

Alderman Wraith 1948. Sixth Form Prefects.

During 1948 there were 583 pupils on the school role. During that year 98 pupils were entered for the Joint Matriculation Board examinations and 74 certificates were awarded. Eight candidates out of fifteen passed the Durham Higher School Certificate.

Alderman Wraith 1948. The Drama Group.
Left to right:
Margaret Lawson, Phoebe Stabler, Jack White and Frank Brown.
Front: Alice Thompson and Barbara Milner.

SPENNYMOOR REMEMBERED - BOOK 3

The following four photographs are from the panoramic whole school photograph which was taken in May 1951. The events of 1951 are recorded from A Jubilee History of the school.

In 1951 Councillor T.Liddle laid the foundation stone of the new Grammar Technical School. In this year the General Certificate of Education replaced the School Certificate. Henceforth, certificates were given for individual subjects and did not depend on a grouped pass. Subjects were sat at two levels: the Ordinary Level, with a standard equivalent to the old Credit standard: and the Advanced level replacing the Higher School certificate.

SPENNYMOOR REMEMBERED - BOOK 3

Eighty-two candidates sat at O Level and 56 gained certificates with four or more subjects. At A level 20 sat and 15 were successful.

The school played its part in the local celebrations for the Festival of Britain by staging a revue entitled "Mine's a Miner," taking as its theme, Coal.

The school camp was to Clawdd in North Wales, the usual 200 boys and girls with staff being taken during the summer holidays. At Easter a party went to Paris, the first foreign trip since the war. Another party went to London to see the Festival of Britain exhibition.

SPENNYMOOR REMEMBERED - BOOK 3

Alderman Wraith Boy's Gymnastic Team.
The photograph was taken on speech night 1950, the teacher in charge is Joe Coulthard who started teaching at the school in 1949.
Among others: G. Richardson, D. Ghent, G. Berriman, N. Morten, J. Robinson, P.Benson, D. Leathley, E. Simpson, R. Bell, A. Murray, J. Oxenham., A. Hood, J.Wells, R. Pearce and T.Blenkin.

Joe Coulthard.

Joe was a native of West Auckland, after attending Bishop Auckland Grammar School he went to the City of Leeds College where he won his colours at football and gymnastics. Two years after the start of the war he joined the R.A.F. and served five years as a physical training instructor. When he was demobbed in 1946 he taught for a while at Kimblesworth County School and in 1947 went to Carnegie College were he obtained a diploma in physical education. After leaving Carnegie he taught at Whinney Hill and then in 1949 he began his teaching career at Spennymoor Alderman Wraith and Spennymoor Grammar Technical School.

Joe had played football for West Auckland before the war but after he joined Bishop Auckland where he played as wing-half. After returning from Carnegie he signed for Shildon and played there as full-back until he retired from the game in 1951.

I first met Joe when I transferred from Broom Cottages Modern School into the sixth form of Spennymoor Grammar Technical School, in September 1956. What a revelation it was going into a modern school building. The sporting facilities were outstanding; a purpose built gymnasium, showers and proper changing facilities, but even better was the programme of physical activities that was available. In the two years that I was at the school I was able to participate in football, cricket, hockey, rugby, basketball and gymnastics, which made a welcome, break from the studying. Joe was a good teacher well liked and respected, he was strict but fair, a gentleman.

SPENNYMOOR REMEMBERED - BOOK 3

Spennymoor Grammar Technical School 1955
Among others: Fred Cook, Stan Graham, Ron Egglestone, Brian Siddle, George Scarlet, Dick Harvey, Derek Oswald, Harry Lennon.
Barbara Rand, Jim Ellison, John Callander, David Miller
Joy Ashton, Ann Leonard.

Spennymoor Grammar Technical School.
The school choir 1955.

SPENNYMOOR REMEMBERED - BOOK 3

Middlestone Moor School c.1890. Shortly to be demolished the pupils being transferred to the newly built school in Rock Road.

Spennymoor West Infants 1962.
Destroyed in the disastrous fire and replaced by a new school to accommodate both infants and juniors.

SPENNYMOOR REMEMBERED - BOOK 3

Spennymoor West Modern School Staff c.1970.
Back Row: Anne Ramshaw, Connie Hodgson, Alan Smith, John Henry, Gregg Briggs, Bob Ablwy, Harry Hodgson, Cynthia Turnbull, and Yvonne Jones.
Front Row: Jim Carr, Winnie Coia, Peggy Langstaff, Eddy Lake, Dick Anderson, Winnie Newlands, Edna Foster and Maude Hutchinson.

Spennymoor West Dancers c.1964.
Among others: Julie Parkinson, Eunice Dunn, Gail Russel, Susan Parkinson, Elsie Littlefair, Kathleen Ellis, Brenda Dunn, Barbara Beasley and Shiela Thomas.

SPENNYMOOR REMEMBERED - BOOK 3

Spennymoor West Girls Hockey Team 1966-67
Among others: Julie Howe, Mrs. Hodgson, Jane Card, Barbara Jewitt, Janice Gibson, Kathleen Pennick, Brenda Dunn, Anne Marshall, Sheila Howe, Audrey Noble and Margaret Curry.

Spennymoor West A Team 1966-67. D.Wayman, J.Summerson, K.Leybourne, K.Galloway, K.Richardson, J.Robson, D.Littlefair, H.Murphy, A.Grey, P.Storey, J.Gibbons, E.Foster, J.Hodgson, K.Henderson, J.Smith and Mr.Hodgson.

SPENNYMOOR REMEMBERED - BOOK 3

North Road Juniors Football Team 1970.
Back Row: John Allison, Kenneth Burtinshaw, Raymond Crosby, Michael Bostock, Geoffrey Cant, Brian Liddle, Trevor Craddock, Eric Famulock.
Front Row: Anthony Bostock, Keith Metcalfe, Kevin Lamb, Kevin Cowan, David Griffen, David Franks and Mr. Potts.

I started playing for the team mainly to get out of school early on away matches. For home matches I was sent out early to make sure the footballs were laced up properly and were all at the right pressure. I remember that we had a strong and successful team, we were rarely beaten at home because we were used to playing on our 45-degree sloping pitch. It sloped from wing to wing rather than end to end; the visitors couldn't get used to the odd experience. I also remember the short journey over the "battery" to play St. Charles School. I would be standing on the goal line watching the two teams going up and down as they ran backwards and forwards on the uneven pitch.

Michael Bostock (junior), goalkeeper.

SPENNYMOOR REMEMBERED - BOOK 3

North Road Boys c.1950, Mr. Ellison's Class.
Among others: Barry Wilson, Bobby Relph, Sam Bartram, Melvyn Roundsley, Billy Davis, Bert Beavis, Bart Bambridge, David Button, Tommy Blair, Fred Birbeck, Raymond Petch, John Hetherington, Dave Savage, Tom Ward, Derek Lindsay, Frank Clements and Bevin Easter.

North Road Junior Mixed School c.1958.
Mrs. Tuck, Miss Wilson and Mrs. Simpson.

SPENNYMOOR REMEMBERED - BOOK 3

North Road Junior Mixed c.1958.
Miss Fishburn, Mr. Gregson and Miss Wright.

Tudhoe National Boys AFC 1907-08
A.Pitchard, W.Scott, K.Troupe, T.Robinson, J.Catheral, T.Brabban.
D.Troupe, D.Marshall, R. Howe, R.Ainsley, A.Crago, J.Keers.
J.Troupe, J.Robinson, W.Moreland, R.Wood, E. Riley, C.Milburn, J.Wright.

SPENNYMOOR REMEMBERED - BOOK 3

Tudhoe St. Charles Football Team 1935.

Winners of the Weardale Cup which was presented by the Weardale Steel Coal and Coke Company and competed for every year
Left to right
Back Row: L. Scanlon, A Jackson, Mr. H. Hanratty (headmaster), J. A. McNulty (sports master), R. Cameron and A. Pickering.
Seated: G. Robinson, W. Murray, K. Donnelly, J. Murray, and J. Scorer.
Front seated: L. McGough and W. Cleary.

The beaten team was from Middlestone Moor school. The game had been played on the Good Templars pitch at Tudhoe Colliery. The Good Templar's Hall was on the site that Tudhoe Workman's Club is built on now, the playing field was where Oval Park is now. The winners were presented with a solid silver medal each with their name engraved on it.

Just over the school wall you can see the top of Rington's Tea van which was making a delivery in Durham Road.

The Good Templars or to give them their full title, the International Order of Good Templars had a football team of their own, which played regularly on the field. The teams changed in the big wooden hut, which was the Temperance Hall.

Jack Murray

SPENNYMOOR REMEMBERED - BOOK 3

Tudhoe St. Charles Football Team 1932-33.
Among others:: Sep Hall, John Donkin, R. Drake, Billy Kelly and Mr. McNulty.

Tudhoe Colliery School Football Team 1932.
Among others, left to right:
Back Row: E. Moyle, Mr. Platts, J. Simpson, G. Wregglesworth, and K. Lowery
Middle Row: Eddy, Thompson, J. White, S. Adams and H. Kirkup.
Front Row: J. Deakin and P. Joyce.

SPENNYMOOR REMEMBERED - BOOK 3

King Street Girls at Robin Hood's Bay c. 1950

King Street School Football Team 1928.
Among others: John Southall and Frederick Hamilton

SPENNYMOOR REMEMBERED - BOOK 3

Spennymoor and District Teachers' Association

Souvenir Programme

OF THE

"Welcome Home" Gathering,

To all Teachers in the Spennymoor Education District who served with the Colours during the course of the World-War, 1914 to 1919.

TO BE HELD IN THE

TOWN HALL, SPENNYMOOR,

ON THURSDAY, MAY 8th, 1919, AT 7 P.M.

(1) PROGRESSIVE WHIST.
(2) LIGHT REFRESHMENTS.
(3) ADDRESSES BY:
   (a) Alderman R. Richardson, M.P., Chairman, (Durham County Education Committee.)
   (b) A. J. Dawson, Esq., Director of Education, (Durham County Education Committee.)
(4) VOTES OF THANKS.
(5) DANCE.

JOS. W. R. MASON, President.
JAS. W. ROYSTON, Hon. Sec.

LIST OF DISTINCTIONS GAINED

CLOUGH, T., (1) M.S.M. (2) Crose di Guerra (Italian).
O'DONNELL, M. F., (1) M.M. (2) La Medaille Militaire (France).
PHILIPSON, T., M.M.
POTTS, J. J., M.M.
SANDERSON, C. (late), (1) D.S.O. (2) Russian Order of St. George
WELSH, T., M.C.
WILMER, C., M.C.

IN MEMORIAM

Killed in Action or Died of Wounds

FOR

HUMANITY, CIVILISATION, LIBERTY.

"Who dies if England lives?
Who lives if England dies?"

ARNETT, W.
BAILES, W. H.
BAKER, W.
BROWN, W. L. G.
CHIPCASE, H.
CORNER, A.
FAIRLESS, E.
FERGUSON, T.
MACPHERSON, G.
ROBINSON, T. N.
SANDERSON, C.
TURNER, A.
WAKE, J. P.

REPORTED MISSING.

DEIGHTON, R.   MOORE, H.

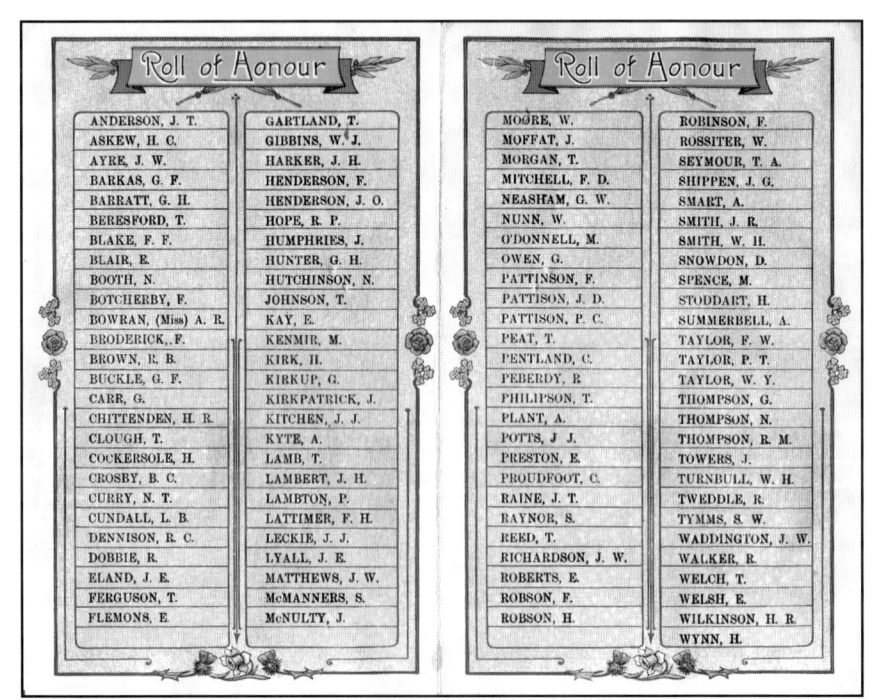

Roll of Honour

ANDERSON, J. T.	GARTLAND, T.
ASKEW, H. C.	GIBBINS, W. J.
AYRE, J. W.	HARKER, J. H.
BARKAS, G. F.	HENDERSON, F.
BARRATT, G. H.	HENDERSON, J. O.
BERESFORD, T.	HOPE, R. P.
BLAKE, F. F.	HUMPHRIES, J.
BLAIR, E.	HUNTER, G. H.
BOOTH, N.	HUTCHINSON, N.
BOTCHERBY, F.	JOHNSON, T.
BOWRAN, (Miss) A. R.	KAY, E.
BRODERICK, F.	KENMIR, M.
BROWN, R. B.	KIRK, H.
BUCKLE, G. F.	KIRKUP, G.
CARR, G.	KIRKPATRICK, J.
CHITTENDEN, H. R.	KITCHEN, J. J.
CLOUGH, T.	KYTE, A.
COCKERSOLE, H.	LAMB, T.
CROSBY, B. C.	LAMBERT, J. H.
CURRY, N. T.	LAMBTON, P.
CUNDALL, L. B.	LATTIMER, F. H.
DENNISON, R. C.	LECKIE, J. J.
DOBBIE, R.	LYALL, J. E.
ELAND, J. E.	MATTHEWS, J. W.
FERGUSON, T.	McMANNERS, S.
FLEMONS, E.	McNULTY, J.

MOORE, W.	ROBINSON, F.
MOFFAT, J.	ROSSITER, W.
MORGAN, T.	SEYMOUR, T. A.
MITCHELL, F. D.	SHIPPEN, J. G.
NEASHAM, G. W.	SMART, A.
NUNN, W.	SMITH, J. R.
O'DONNELL, M.	SMITH, W. H.
OWEN, G.	SNOWDON, D.
PATTINSON, F.	SPENCE, M.
PATTISON, J. D.	STODDART, H.
PATTISON, P. C.	SUMMERBELL, A.
PEAT, T.	TAYLOR, F. W.
PENTLAND, C.	TAYLOR, P. T.
PEBERDY, R.	TAYLOR, W. Y.
PHILIPSON, T.	THOMPSON, G.
PLANT, A.	THOMPSON, N.
POTTS, J. J.	THOMPSON, R. M.
PRESTON, E.	TOWERS, J.
PROUDFOOT, C.	TURNBULL, W. H.
RAINE, J. T.	TWEDDLE, R.
RAYNOR, S.	TYMMS, S. W.
REED, T.	WADDINGTON, J. W.
RICHARDSON, J. W.	WALKER, R.
ROBERTS, E.	WELCH, T.
ROBSON, F.	WELSH, E.
ROBSON, H.	WILKINSON, H. R.
	WYNN, H.

Spennymoor Teachers who served in the First World War.

THREE

BYERS GREEN

Byers Green is a much more ancient place than Spennymoor, it has been a place of habitation for many hundreds of years. Earliest records show it first being mentioned in the Boldon Book of 1183. The Boldon book was a land survey carried out by Hugh Pudsey the then Bishop of Durham. There are three theories as to how the name Byers Green originated;
1. that it originated from the Anglo Saxon word *Bearwas* meaning 'The Woods' or 'The Wooded Hills'. This explanation is disputed because another translation of *Bearwas* is 'wheelbarrow.'
2. that the word Byers is from either the Anglo-Saxon *byre* a small mound; or *byre* a cattle stall.
3. that *Byr* is another form of the personal Anglo-Saxon name *Beorht* and therefore the meaning might be 'Beorht's Green.'

Byers Green was a secluded rural settlement, until the advent of mining in the area, being cut off from the surrounding area by the River Wear. There was no bridge and the only means of crossing the River was by ferry.

Byers Green Hoppings
During the 17th. and 18th Centuries Byers Green was famous for its Annual Hopping apparently it was renowned throughout the County as the following extract from the poem Byers Green Hopping by Mathew Richley recounts.

"We have to louse te day at neun;
An'mak'oursels both smart an'clean
An'then be off te Byers Green,
For lads an'lasses fra all parts
Will gan te-day in gigs an' carts;
Some will their frisky nags bestride,

SPENNYMOOR REMEMBERED – BOOK 3

An'others will on donkeys ride;
While some there be, whe will be there,
Will have te gan on "Shankey's Mare;"
For folk will come fra miles about
Te join this merry village rout,
Fra Merrington an' Ferry Hill,
Fra Willington an' Furnace Mill,
Fra Coundon, and fra Shildon te,
The folk will flock the fun to see;
Fra Hunwick, and fra distant Creuk,
They'll cum te drink, an'dance, an'smuke;
Fra Sunnybrow an'Seldomseen,
They all will cum te Byers Green;
E'en Auclan', with its pride an'trade,
Will help te swell the cavalcade.

Hoppings were originally religious in character and probably based on earlier pagan festivals, however, the religious intentions were soon forgotten, and feasting, dancing and other sports soon took the place of the original religious theme. The name "hopping," a North Country word is derived from the hopping and dancing that took place at them. Despite the Act of Convocation passed during the reign of Henry VIII to restrict them they still continued in out of the way places like Byers Green.

In the preamble to his poem, Mathew Richley has this to say about the Byers Green Hopping:

" As evidence of the popularity of Byers Green Hopping half a century ago (1830), it may be stated that an Auckland worthy, noted for his love of field sports, attended it for fifty consecutive years. It was the custom of the village matrons to make gooseberry pies for the entertainment of their friends; and at each of the inns a Hopping pie was also made, and it was considered an honour to be allowed to cut and serve it out, and one which was frequently conferred upon the worthy above noticed. When any of the young folk in the village (either lad or lass) went off to country service, a condition was always put in the agreement between them and their masters, that they should have a holiday at the hopping. The influx of the mining population, however, introduced an element of modern sporting into the rural simplicity of former days, which caused the promoters to give it up, so that Byers Green Hopping is now (1879) numbered among the things of the past."

Thomas Wright.

Thomas Wright is perhaps the most famous of all Byers Green inhabitants. He was born in the village in 1711 and despite his humble beginnings Thomas developed into a man with wide and ranging interests. He became famous as an astronomer and a mathematician but he was also a mathematical instrument maker, a garden designer, architect and an author. He wrote and published several books and was regarded as the absolute authority on many of the topics he wrote about. He was responsible for building the Folly at Westerton, which was constructed to aid his study of astronomy. In 1756 he settled in the village rebuilding the original family house and he remained there until his death in 1786.

SPENNYMOOR REMEMBERED – BOOK 3

Thomas Wright

Ruin of Thomas Wrights House.
This photograph was taken in 1966 prior to demolition. It shows the back of the house and the sorry state that it had been brought to by vandalism. As well as being the home of Thomas Wright in more recent years it had been owned by Peggy Hutchinson who was well known for making and writing about home made wines. During her time there she had tried unsuccessfully to get the building officially listed and preserved because of its historic interest.

Byers Green Colliery 1908.
Byers Green Colliery was established in 1840 as a result of the building of the Byers Green Branch Railway of the Clarence Railway Company. Although coal deposits had been known to exist in the area for some considerable time there had been no effective means of transport to get the coal to market.

Byers Green Colliery Coke Ovens.
The opening of the colliery brought in a large influx of miners and their families the population increasing from 207 in 1831 to 1,025 in 1851. The Michael Pit closed in 1892 and the pit closed altogether in 1929.

SPENNYMOOR REMEMBERED – BOOK 3

Byers Green School c.1860.
The school was situated halfway down the High Street and was sometime known as the dame school. In more recent times Robinsons used it as a coalyard

Byers Green School Class 5 c.1919.
The only pupil identified is Matty Robinson who is sitting to the right of the board.

SPENNYMOOR REMEMBERED – BOOK 3

Byers Green Senior School Group 3 c. 1900.
Hutchinson Robinson is the fourth from the left in the second row from the back..

Institute Street.
This photograph and the following two were used in a court case to settle the ownership of some land in the early 1900's.

SPENNYMOOR REMEMBERED – BOOK 3

The location of these photographs is likely to be one of the small streets, which ran off Institute Street i.e. behind the stretch of High Street, which lay, between the Institute and the Methodist Chapel.

SPENNYMOOR REMEMBERED – BOOK 3

Byers Green Water Carnival 1908.
A composite photograph of the various events that took place at the Water Carnival or Gala. The carnival was an annual event and it is not certain when they first took place but they continued up until about the beginning of the First World War. Alf Todd can remember being at one when he was about four years old but cannot remember any after that, therefore, this would place the last one to be held in 1914.

General View of the Water Carnival of 1908.
Note the wooden staging built so far across the river. It was an extremely popular event and people attended from miles around.

SPENNYMOOR REMEMBERED – BOOK 3

Quoits at the 1908 Water Carnival.
The tall contestant on the left waiting to take his turn is Bob Nelson, he had a son called John Tom. The house on the other side of the river was where the ferryman lived. You crossed the river here if you wanted to go to Willington or Crook. See the girls on the right dressed in their Edwardian finery.

'Old Waterloo' c.1910.
Old waterloo was the cannon, which was used to start the canoe races at the Water Carnival. It belonged to Jack Hambling and was kept by Tommy Harrison of Harrison House in a building near his house. Robert Paley was the starter who fired the cannon. Note the police officer at the back. Jack Hambling, the local schoolmaster is thought to be the man at the front right.

SPENNYMOOR REMEMBERED – BOOK 3

The Greathead Family c. 1918.

Byers Green has always had a strong tradition for fetes and carnivals beginning with the hoppings and carrying through to the water carnivals. Another annual event which has taken place over countless years was the Village Carnival which still takes place every year. Above we can see the Greathead family enjoying the occasion in 1918.

Mrs. Greathead is with the children Bobby and Harriet (in plane) and Tom sitting with his mother. Mr. Greathead is on the right with his son John. The plane was made up from old bike parts and apparently was pedalled and pushed halfway across the field on this carnival occasion and then disintigrated

Mr. Greathead was the village barber and a bit of an inventor apparently he developed a prototype for traffic lights, which he had hung up in the house to demonstrate. Unfortunately, so it's said, someone else patented the idea and Mr. Greathead lost out.

SPENNYMOOR REMEMBERED – BOOK 3

Village Carnival c.1930.

Well known character Mrs. T. Barkers and children all dressed up for the Carnival.

Village Carnival c.1935

Left to right:
Robby Littlefair, Alf Todd and Billy Hopps.

We walked to Newfield and back in procession and then we went round the pubs drinking in fancy dress. I was wearing shoes with raised heels and by the time we'd finished I was just about crippled.

Alf Todd

SPENNYMOOR REMEMBERED – BOOK 3

Jubilee 1910.
Byers Green High Street, the houses were decorated for the Silver Jubilee of the King Edward and Queen Mary, many houses in the village were decorated in celebration. The lady on the left was Mrs. Carr.

Tom Southeron c. 1930.

Tom Southeron, landlord, standing at the bar of the Royal Oak in Byers Green.

Byers Green Cricket Team c. 1910.
The only person identified is again the schoolmaster Jack Hambling first left in the back row.

Byers Green Football Team c.1910.
Among Others: Jack Dickinson, Goalkeeper Barley Peart, Ambrose Peart, Jack Brumell, Joe Sheldon and Billy Wheatman

SPENNYMOOR REMEMBERED – BOOK 3

Byers Green United Season 1919 – 1920.
Among others Roxborough, Sidney Snowdon, Hutchinson Robinson, Charlie Mould and Lance Wheatman.

The Orton Family and Others c.1910
Left to Right.

Back Row: Hodgson and Honeywell

Middle Row: Tommy Orton, Head of Byers Green school, daughter Althea and Mrs. Orton.

Front Row: Ada Whitehead (emigrated to Canada) and Kate Todd.

Watson Family of Granville Terrace, Binchester Blocks c.1920.
Left to Right:
Back: Mrs. Watson, Mr. Watson (fitter at Binchester Colliery), Mrs. Pearson (daughter of Byers Green undertaker).
Front: Alan Watson, Nanny Pearson and Charlie Watson.

Four Byers Green Stalwarts c.1920.
Left to Right:
Back:
Dick Robinson (butcher), Bob Haggie (builder)

Front:
Dick Binks (fish shop owner), and Simcock.

Group of Byers Green Men and Boys c.1920.

On the extreme right is Tom Harrison of Harrison House. He was the keeper of the cannon and the canoes that were used for the water carnivals. Tom was a real character, almost a hermit. He kept and allowed all sorts of animals to free range in his house, there were mice, hens, cats and geese feeding on the scraps that he left about for them. Tom was said to be greatly upset when one of the cats killed a mouse, he obviously believed in the theory of live and let live. He had a dovecote in the eves of his house but had no access to it. Alf Todd can remember asking him to sell him a pigeon and being given the following reply: "I owes neebody nowt, I neither buys nor sells, nor borrows nor lends so aad away yer young buggers."

When the 'shows' used to come to Byers green for the village carnival, they used to set up in the field opposite Harrison House. Alf Todd can remember Crow's and Culine's setting up their attractions on the site. Alf's father was a butcher in Byers green and he can remember the show people coming to get their meals at the butcher's shop. In later years the field was used for the Royal Oak Leek Show, now there are houses built on the site.

SPENNYMOOR REMEMBERED – BOOK 3

Harry and Jack Jolly.

These brothers worked as drawers at Byers Green Coke Works. Jack was part owner of the picture house in Byers Green. Both brothers were keen pigeon fanciers.

Storey Family and Others c.1940

Left to Right:
Arthur Sheldon – drove Jewitt's buses and was a well-known pianist around the pubs in Spennymoor.
Robert Davison – his father was a good foot-runner in the village.
Johnston Storey - mechanic for Jewitt's buses.
Alan Storey - son of Johnson.
George Story - caretaker of Spennymoor Shopping Precinct
Billy Storey.

SPENNYMOOR REMEMBERED – BOOK 3

Frank Goundry's Coal Wagon c. 1923.
Left to Right: Bobby Johnson, Frank Goundry and Billy Cole.

Frank Goundry of Wilkinson Street had his own coal business, it only lasted a year as Frank was driving his own bus at the same time and the workload became too much. He started his bus service by converting his coal wagon to a dual-purpose vehicle.

Byers Green and Binchester Men on Holiday.
Among others: Billy Thompson (bandmaster), Tommy Harle, Charlie Briggs, Ralph Slater (bare fist fighter), Matty Groves (Matty one of the few who could read used to sit and read the captions at the silent films for those who couldn't read), and Bob Pattison.

St. Peter's Church Choir c. 1915

The choir was some thirty strong in those days and there they are all dressed up for the village carnival as a band of gypsies. Alf Todd, who was five years old at that time, remembers that the choir walked round the village singing accompanied by a barrel organ. Alf had the privilege of turning the handle. The group was photographed on the tennis court outside the old vicarage.

Among others:

The Rev. Francis Loxley, his two young sons are in the front row, teacher Harriet, Mrs. Pearson, Gerty Whitehead, Kate Todd, Alf Booth, Althea Whitehead, Jimmy Midgely, Mr. Orton

St. Peters Byers Green c. 1912

The Church is in the early English style and was erected in 1844 and consecrated in 1845. A parsonage was added in 1855 It was restored and renovated between 1873 and

SPENNYMOOR REMEMBERED – BOOK 3

1890 and could seat 350 people. At the time the photograph was taken the living was a Rectory with an annual net valeue of £316, with a residence and 4 1/2 acres of glebe.

The Rectors shown in the photograph from left to right are:

1845 James Watson
1875 Robert Eli Hooppell
1897 John Crennell
1898 Percival Young Knight
1902 Francis Edwin Loxley.

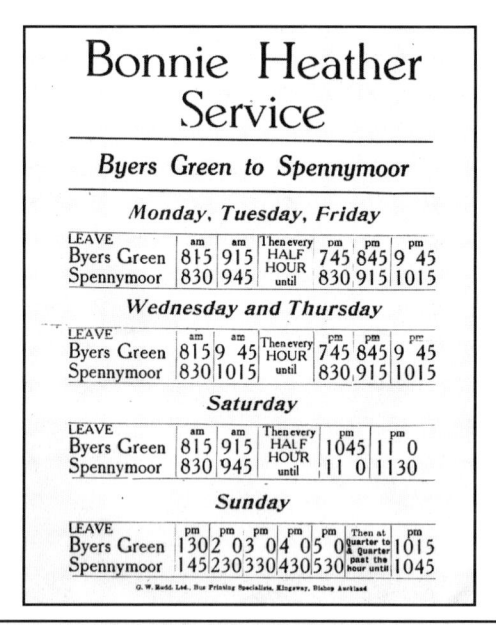

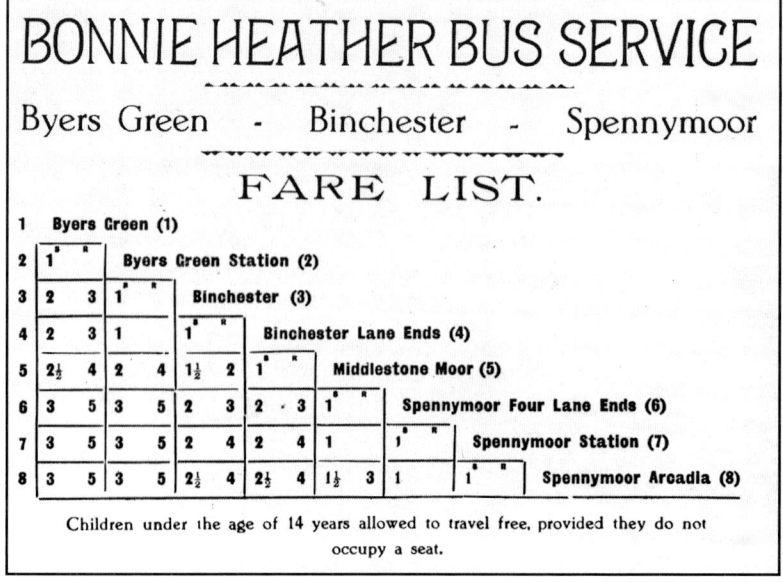

Bonnie Heather Service

Byers Green to Spennymoor

Monday, Tuesday, Friday

LEAVE	am	am	Then every	pm	pm	pm
Byers Green	815	915	HALF HOUR until	745	845	9 45
Spennymoor	830	945		830	915	1015

Wednesday and Thursday

LEAVE	am	am	Then every	pm	pm	pm
Byers Green	815	9 45	HOUR until	745	845	9 45
Spennymoor	830	1015		830	915	1015

Saturday

LEAVE	am	am	Then every	pm	pm
Byers Green	815	915	HALF HOUR until	1045	11 0
Spennymoor	830	945		11 0	1130

Sunday

LEAVE	pm	pm	pm	pm	pm	Then at a Quarter past the hour until	pm
Byers Green	130	2 03	04	05	0		1015
Spennymoor	145	230	330	430	530		1045

G. W. Redd Ltd., Bus Printing Specialists, Kingsway, Bishop Auckland

BONNIE HEATHER BUS SERVICE

Byers Green - Binchester - Spennymoor

FARE LIST.

1	Byers Green (1)
2	1	Byers Green Station (2)
3	2	1	Binchester (3)
4	2	3	1	Binchester Lane Ends (4)
5	2½	4	2	1½	Middlestone Moor (5)
6	3	5	3	5	2	3	2 · 3	1	Spennymoor Four Lane Ends (6)
7	3	5	3	5	2	4	2	4	1	Spennymoor Station (7)
8	3	5	3	5	2½	4	2½	4	1½	3	1	Spennymoor Arcadia (8)

Children under the age of 14 years allowed to travel free, provided they do not occupy a seat.

SPENNYMOOR REMEMBERED – BOOK 3

FOUR

PEOPLE AND EVENTS

Butchers Guild Outing c.1910.
Spennymoor and Bishop Auckland butchers outside the County Hotel in King Street. The bus is a United and would be in a distinctive yellow livery. Third from the left in the front row is James Brass who started his butchering business in Drake Street in 1890.

SPENNYMOOR REMEMBERED – BOOK 3

County Hotel Touring Party c. 1945.
Among others: Jimmy Johnson, 'Anty' Thompson, Mr. Hardy, and Dick Porter.

Crown Touring Party in Blackpool c.1960.
Among others: Jack Sawley, Doug Smith, Mr. Eltringham, Jimmy Grayson, Denny Grayson, Bill Simmonds, Jacky Hopper, Tony Stephenson, Norman Minto and John Cadman

SPENNYMOOR REMEMBERED – BOOK 3

Queens Head Trip to Blackpool, October 1955.

Tudhoe Victory Club Old Mens Trip c.1945.
Among others: Joe Hindmarch, Mr. Pickering, Jack Hodgson, Mr. Heseltine, Roger Paul, Ralph Gray, Alec Hodgson, Danny Jones, Jack Nelson, Billy White and Frank Dixon.

SPENNYMOOR REMEMBERED – BOOK 3

Colliery Inn, Tudhoe Colliery, trip to Blackpool c.1958.
Among others: John Pickford, Bill Morris, Douglas Burnip, Fred Danes, Harry Hodgson, Tossa Toase, John Chatterton, Jake Rowcroft, Tom Davison, Ronnie Robson, Eric Richardson, Jack Davison, Brian Morris, Richie Morris, Peter Morris, Bob Rowcroft, Jacky Kay, Douglas Longstaff, Ray Fairly, Ray Meale, Ralph Maughan, Tot Fairly, Ronnie Fairly, Jack Kay (landlord), Herbert Pickford, Herbert Denny, Ivan Rowcroft and Billy Bowden.

Spennymoor Lads at Butlins c. 1960.
Left to right: Neil Kelley, Francis Smith, Eric Plant, Tommy Dawson, and Teddy Eddington.

SPENNYMOOR REMEMBERED – BOOK 3

Spennymoor Working Men's Club Trip c. 1950
Among others: Jimmy O'Hara, Tom Graham, Teddy Atchison, Abe Showler and Pat Laidler.

Spennymoor Cadets at Barnard Castle 1943.
Among others: Mr. Nunn and Mr. Parker (teachers from King Street School), the Nichol brothers, Billy Wallace, Alan Dowdell and Ray Hirst

    The Spennymoor cadet force was first formed in 1942 at King Street School. It was formed by Mr. Nunn who taught at the school. They met twice a week in a wooden hut beside the school, next to the wooden hut Fish Shop. They were known as the

13th.Battalion. Another detachment was formed at St. Charles school by Mr. Hannratty, this was the 14th.Battalion.

13th. Battalion Drums and Bugles at Bishop Drill Hall 1948.
Among others: Dennis Hardwick, Ray Hardwick, Michael Bostock, Edgar Wallace, Bob Richmond and Jimmy Simpson.

The band was originally formed by Bob Richmond who can be seen in the centre of the picture with his drum. At this time he was sergeant major.

I joined the cadets in 1943, when I was a pupil at King Street School. You had to be at least 13 tears 9 months before you could join. We were issued with trousers, jacket, hat and badge, if you wanted any other equipment you provided them yourself. It cost 15 shillings if you wanted to but a pair of boots. Normally you stayed in the cadets until you were 18 and then left to join the regular army or the Territorials, because I was a pitman I was allowed to stop on in the cadet force to become an instructor. In all I was in the cadet force for 21 years achieving the rank of senior Sergeant Major in the 13th. Battalion. After 12 years as an instructor I received a medal and a citation for the work that I had done in the cadet force.

When I first started as an instructor it was on a voluntary basis, but later I was paid. When payment started the ranks of the cadet force was boosted dramatically. The Spennymoor detachment grew to be one of the biggest in the battalion.. We were always short of money and consequently everything had to be done on the cheap. When we started the band we had to provide our own instruments, and raised money by jumble sales and raffles. When we went to camp we had to provide everything ourselves, rations, tents and any other gear that we needed. When we competed against other cadet forces we had to pay all our own expenses. I remember we once took a boxing team to London, we went by bus and the lads virtually got off the bus and into the ring with obvious results. We found out later that our opponents had been there for three days prior to the competition.. Despite the lack of funds we always did our best, we were triers and got a lot of enjoyment out of it.

Bob Richmond.

SPENNYMOOR REMEMBERED – BOOK 3

13th. Battalion Football Team 1945. The photograph was taken at Page Bank. Among others: Terry Sinclair, Billy Moor, Michael Bostock, Jack Davison, Bob Richmond, Ray Hardwick, Dennis Hardwick, Billy Walker and Harry Boyes.

I joined the cadets in 1946, when I was 12. We met twice a week in the drill hut at King Street School. There were quite a few of us, Dicky Freeman, Ray Hardwick, Dennis Hardwick, Billy Moor, Harry Boyes, Edgar Wallace, Tommy Marriat, Jacky Thompson, Tommy Bowes and George Simpson are some names I can remember.

There were lots of activities to take part in, most of them sporting. We had a football team, running team, boxing team and wrestling team. We played football locally about once a month. We weren't in a league we just played friendlies against other cadets and local church teams. We competed in the other sports when we went to the monthly camp at Whitburn and when we went to the annual camp at Kingston-upon-Hull. I was also a member of the band, I was a sergeant and played the drums. We used to practice our marching on King Street Schoolyard, Dicky Freeman I remember was brilliant at gun twirling.

We used to hold manoeuvres in Tudhoe woods, the enemy usually being the other local cadet group, these sometimes used to end up in fights. We also had to do endurance exercises up in Weardale near Stanhope. We used to march up there from Spennymoor, we were given basic rations and were expected to supplement these by living off the countryside. We were given 20 rounds of live .22 ammunition and were expected to shoot rabbits, I don't think anyone managed to kill a one. We also set snares unsuccessfully but we did manage to catch fish out of the river. Each individual had to take turns at running the camp, the biggest job being to feed everybody, we had a big cooking pot and everything went into it. We had a great time but once the camp was called to order the discipline was very strict.   Michael Bostock (senior)

Accident in King Street .1970.

The accident occurred when the car travelling at speed from the direction of Bessemer Park tried to beat the landrover, which was crossing from Barnfield Road into Cheapside. As you can see it didn't make it, fortunately no one was seriously hurt, the two youths in the car ran off from the scene of the accident and it later turned out that the car was stolen.

SPENNYMOOR REMEMBERED – BOOK 3

Carl Grey.
Carl Grey was a well know musician who used to play frequently at the Rink during its heyday. He was a versatile musician as can be seen from the range of instruments he could play.

Rink Dance Band 1940.
Left to right:
Bill Ovingham (trombone), Dacre Long (trumpet), Eric Whittle (trumpet), Randal Wallace (2nd. Alto Sax.), Jack Goodie (1st. alto Sax.), "Saxie" Eccles (tenor Sax.), Joe Proudlock (drums) and Bill Robson (piano).

SPENNYMOOR REMEMBERED – BOOK 3

Rink Dance Band 1940's
Among others: Charley Stott (drums), Bobby Hepple (trumpet), Carl Grey (saxophone) and Dave Emmerson the manager of the Rink.

Spennymoor Temperance Band
Jimmy Grieves is in the front row, third from the left.

Army Service Corps 1914.
Bottom left Norman Minnis also third from right second row from the back Tommy White who had a grocery shop in Merrington Lane.

Norman Minnis.

Norman was one of the first pupils to attend the Higher Elementary School in Spennymoor. He ran away from school at the age of 14 and joined the army, you can see from the photograph that he is very young looking. He was sent to Salonika but was brought back after the intervention of his parents.

He worked in the mines in the Spennymoor area and when old enough joined the Territorial Army, rising to the rank of Company Sgt. Major P.S.I. and was made warrant Officer Class II, in 1933. Prior to the declaration of war in 1939 he recruited young men into the army in Spennymoor one being his son. He left the pit and was transferred into the regular army and was sent to Bowburn to recruit and form a company there.

When war was declared in September 1939 both father and son were sent to France immediately. The son escaped back to England via Dunkirk. Norman formed part of a rearguard action against the Germans to delay them to allow our troops to escape from Dunkirk, he was missing for two years and was finally reported killed on May 20th. 1940.

DLI Officers 1940.
Group of Officers photographed prior to going off to France. Captain Billy Pattullo is second from the right at the back and Captain Jack Kipling seated first left in the front row. Captain Kipling was killed in action a month later in the same rearguard action as Norman Minnis was.

Gardeners at Whitworth Hall c.1925

Central Methodist Church Sunday schools Anniversary 1954.
Among others: David Sodey, Brian Gray, Ian Venice, Gordon Sodey, Alan Waugh, Judith Pinkney, Charlotte Graham, Joan Pritchard, Judith Marshall, Julia Davies, Marjorie Luck and Sandra Hamilton.

St. Paul's Church Garden Party 1940.
The Flower Sellers photographed in the garden of St. Paul's vicarage.
Left to right:
Shirley Willis, Pearl Brown and Edith Robinson.

Farmers and Tradesmen's Dance 1954
Among others; Matt Robinson, Charlie Button, Billy Hunter, Eric Webb, Olwell Robinson, Edith Robinson, Vera Button, Brenda Hunter and Joyce Webb.

St. Patrick's Night Dance. Town Hall 1958.
Left to right: Dorothy Laidler, Walter Illingworth, Janet Brayshaw, Leslie Wise, Bill Laidler, Walter Meek, Brian Illingworth and Clare Illingwort

SPENNYMOOR REMEMBERED – BOOK 3

Green Tree Crowd, Tudhoe Village c.1970.

Edward Norman Vincent. 1934-35 Season.

Eddy Vincent a well-known local footballer from Tudhoe colliery. Eddy played for Spennymoor before going to Grimsby Town and the Stockport County, At one time he earned £1,200 in a year. He was nicknamed "Chopper" Vincent because of his strong play and his ability to break up attacks.

> Tudhoe Colliery,
> Spennymoor.
>
> 8th, March 1939.
>
> Dear Eddy,
>
> Your friends of Tudhoe are very pleased at the magnificent manner in which you and your Clubmates are progressing in the Cup, and whilst appreciating the enormous task you have been asked to overcome in meeting the Wolves, feel confident that you will reach the Final and carry the trophy back to Grimsby.
>
> We are proud of the fact that we have at least one, who was bred and born amongst us, who will take part in these great matches and we wish you the very best of luck.
>
> Whether in success or failure we sincerely hope that you will attain those heights of greatness we know you are capable of, and, by so doing, add yet another name to that already long list of grand sportsmen of Dear Old Tudhoe.
>
> Yours Sincerely,
>
> Jack Thompson

Letter of Support sent to Eddy Vincent 1939.
The people who signed the letter were members of Tudhoe Victory Club.

SPENNYMOOR REMEMBERED – BOOK 3

St. Andrew's Church Lads Brigade c. 1910.
The bearded gentlemen is Reverend Wykes who later became Canon Wykes. What a stirring scene, cavalry as well as rifles arrayed in front of the group.

Mothers Bible Meeting group 1901.
The Mothers used to meet on Monday afternoons at 2.30 p.m. in the Parish Hall in Cheapside. This must have been a special occasion as the photograph was taken in the garden of the vicarage in North Road. The ladies are well equipped for tennis and croquet.

St. Andrew's Mothers Bible Reading Group 1901.
The photograph was taken in the grounds of the vicarage in North Road.

Caesar Milburn.
Resplendent in his Church Lad's Brigade uniform at the age of 15. A keen member of the Church Lad's Brigade from an early age he was a drummer in St. Andrew's group. He was a regular churchgoer from an early age, he is pictured with his mother on the previous page. He is the child on the extreme right of the photograph.

In later life he was the drummer for Moody's Jazz Band, Moody's Dance Orchestra, the Astoria Band and Whitworth Band. He was a bandsman out in India during WW II when he returned from the war he worked on the railways and worked at Whitworth Pit until he retired.

The Astoria Band.

Dedication of the Cenotaph October, 1919.

SPENNYMOOR REMEMBERED – BOOK 3

Old Wooden Tivoli 1920.
The owner John William Jackson is in the front row with his grandson Jack and his wife, Matilda next to him with their grandson Arthur. Second left in the front row is their daughter Laura with her daughter Mona. Laura's husband John William Jackson is kneeling at left front.

The New Tivoli 1928.
With its wonderful art deco façade the building which replaced the wooden building after it had burned down.

Combined Tivoli and Town Hall Kinema Staff. 1947.
Photograph taken to commemorate the retirement of Jimmy Bell the manager of the "Tiv" pictured centre.

Town Hall Kinema 1977.
Prior to demolition, the National Provincial Bank, which took up the front ground floor, has already moved to its new site on the new shopping precinct.

Whit Hughes.
Whit Hughes was the official photographer at Spennymoor R.O.F. during the war. He also did free-lance work for the Northern Echo. Occasionally he stood in as manager of the Tivoli. He is seen here with Betty Grayson and Jean Atkinson, who both worked at the Tivoli during the 1940's.

Olga Mitchell c. 1940.
Olga was usherette at the Cambridge Cinema, she is photographed here on the Cambridge stage in the full finery of her uniform.

Olga Mitchell's Wedding Day 1942.
Left to right: Mr. Siddle, June Siddle, Jack Phillips, Olga Mitchell, Percy Gibbs, Nora Botcherby and Herbert Durdle.
Mrs. Durdle and Mrs. Annie Mitchell.

An interesting photograph having a strong connection with the Cambridge Theatre. Olga was born in the Shafto Arms and the family moved from there into the Cambridge during the early 1920's. The family also took over the tenancy of the Theatre as well, both pub and theatre belonged to Vaux the brewers. At this time the Cambridge was a live theatre, and was also a venue for boxing matches.. Due to Mr. Mitchell's failing health the family moved from the Cambridge into the North Eastern Hotel in 1927 and in 1929 Mr. Mitchell died.

Sometime during the 1930's Mrs. Mitchell and her family moved back into the Cambridge Theatre and pub. Eventually the theatre was taken over by the Durdle family by which time live theatre was gone. Sometimes plays and productions were put on but for the most part they showed films. Mr. Durdle was tragically killed in a motor car accident. Mr. and Mrs. Durdle also had the Chocolate Box confectioners' shop on the corner of High Street and Dundas Street.

The cast of Merrie England.
The play was performed in the Cambridge Theatre by Spennymoor Operatic Society during the time that the Mitchells were managers, possibly in 1928.

Cambridge Theatre Poster c. 1895

The Last Train.
The last train to leave Spennymoor goods station on 2nd. May 1966 ending the towns 130 connection with the railways.

Tudhoe Colliery Festive Float c. 1935.
The photograph was taken outside The Gables one of the oldest buildings in the area, which had originally been a farm. The site is now occupied by Tudhoe Workinmen's Club. The adult in the photograph is Old Jack Walker.

SPENNYMOOR REMEMBERED – BOOK 3

Merrington Lane Juniors c. 1950.
Among others: Mattimoe, Williams, Redhead, Stewart, Trotter, Griffith, Smith and Snowball.
The photograph was taken on the old football field in Merrington Lane (next to the Factory. On the day the photo was taken we beat the league champions (Shildon Juniors) 3 – 1 in the first round of the Durham County Cup.

Dave Curle

Merrington Lane Stalwarts c.1925.

Standing left to right:
Joe Mohan, Warbler Walsley, Dickie Kettle and Alf Golightly.

Sitting: Albert Curle, Fred Walters and Freddy Curle.

The photograph was taken outside a beer house, which was just over the railway crossing as you came into Merrington Lane from Coulson Street. There were two or three beer houses in Merrington Lane as well as the pubs. They were licensed to sell only beer and not spirits.

SPENNYMOOR REMEMBERED – BOOK 3

Taken outside Tommy Whites Shop c. 1955.
Left to right: Frank Smith, Bill Connor, Geoffrey Kell and Harry Connor.

Merrington Lane wheelbarrow race c.1930
Among others. From left to right:
Second barrow, Joe Willis (steward of the K.G.H.) pushing the barrow and sitting in it Robert (Gooser) Goundry Fourth barrow, Billy Connor pushing.

SPENNYMOOR REMEMBERED – BOOK 3

Spennymoor Biltonians c. 1930.

Scottish pipe band or "Kiltie" band as it was referred to, established during the 1920's and very popular through to the 1930's.

Among others:
George Grey, Jimmy Grey, Roland grey, Tommy Booth, Jack Angus, Waterworth, Hodgson, Turnbull, Atkinson, Blood, Wood, Jimmy Greaves, Joe Burns, Stan Bestford, Josie Dodds, Tony Jimmison, Jowie Hickson, T. Angus, Joe Angus, Dominic Daley, Kit Bowman, Teddy Campbell, Joe Haley, William Burns, Joe Patterson, Hughes, George Graham, Henderson, Stout and Reg Waggot.

I remember that we used to train along Carr Lane alongside the Park and up to the Pit Head. We used to train twice weekly, which is why we won so many cups marching. On the other hand our music never won many cups. We practised our playing every Sunday above Petty's shop on the end of the Dicey's School, and every Saturday we would march down the High Street before catching our bus to which ever town was holding its carnival that Saturday. We had some marvellous times but too often we used to miss the last bus home and had to walk back to Spennymoor. Nearly every town and village in County Durham had a carnival week in those days. Happy days then back to the local pit on a Monday and back to normal again, getting up and going to work at 1.30 in the morning till 12 o'clock noon.

Reginald Waggot

SPENNYMOOR REMEMBERED – BOOK 3

William Wright.

William Burn, Drum Major.

Funeral Procession along Low Grange Road c. 1920.

SPENNYMOOR REMEMBERED – BOOK 3

Spennymoor Amateur Operatic Society.

"The Gondoliers"

(By permission of R. D'Oyly Carte, Esq.)

TOWN HALL. 14TH—19TH APRIL, 1947.

The Gondoliers Ladies and Men's Chorus.
The following names are taken from the cast list for the chorus:
Ladies: M. Yeoman, M. Tolley, M. Fenwick, G. Harvey, G. Button, Mrs. C. Button, I. Sutton, E. Goodyear. E. Harris, I. King, W. Watson, A. Fisher, M. Hughes, M. Walton, J. Williams, D. Rowley, B. Wendell, F. Baugh, M. Taylor, Mrs. Fairley, Mrs. Kirk and E. Sutton.
Men: C. R. Edwards, N. Harrison, J. Henderson, C. Makinson, R. Maddison, S. Hall, A. Smart, F. Walters, T. Moult, N. Graham, G. Robson, J. Murray, T. Murray, J. Fox, M. Hall, J. Black and C. Button.

The Gondoliers.
S. Martin, G. Goodyear, S. Lee, C. Dennison, A. Cowans and S. Prest.
In the background the old chapel long since demolished, one of the two chapels from which Chapel Street got its name.

Robert Heslop. C.1947.
Robert Heslop was a well-known local artist who was one of the Settlement group of artists along with Norman Cornish, Tom McGuinnes and Herbert Dees. He is shown here with pupils of his art class.

Robert Heslop.
Working on a colliery mural commissioned by Durham County Council.

Billy Liar 1964.
A Settlement Drama Group Production. Left to right: Muriel Lamb, Jim Storey, Sadie Rodgers and June Boden

Celebration 1967.
A Settlement Drama Group production.
BackRow: Terry Robson, Jack Kane, Velma Rawlinson and Barbara Saunders.
Front Row: June Bowden, Edith Kirtley, Trevor Abley and Carrie Johnson.

Settlement Chess Club c. 1964.
On this occasion D. Hempson was playing 20 people at the same time. Among others in the photograph: D. Hempson, Neil Kelly and Martin Darsnicks

Spennymoor Nursery Fire 1969.

SPENNYMOOR REMEMBERED – BOOK 3

Tudhoe Colliery Banner c.1920.
Among others: Harry Dixon, Tommy "Brush" Cadman and Frank Dixon. This banner was replaced in 1921 by one depicting the Village Green at Tudhoe.

Kenmirs Cricket Team. Winners of the Dean and Chapter Novices Cup c. 1955.
Back: Peter Scott, Billy Elliot, Tommy Airy, Freddy Roberts, Arthur Pickering and Dicky Wallace.
Front: Jack Hull, Clive Mason, Laurie Gill, Billy Reavley, Wilf Taylor and George Brydon.

SPENNYMOOR REMEMBERED – BOOK 3

Spennymoor United Football Team 1947.

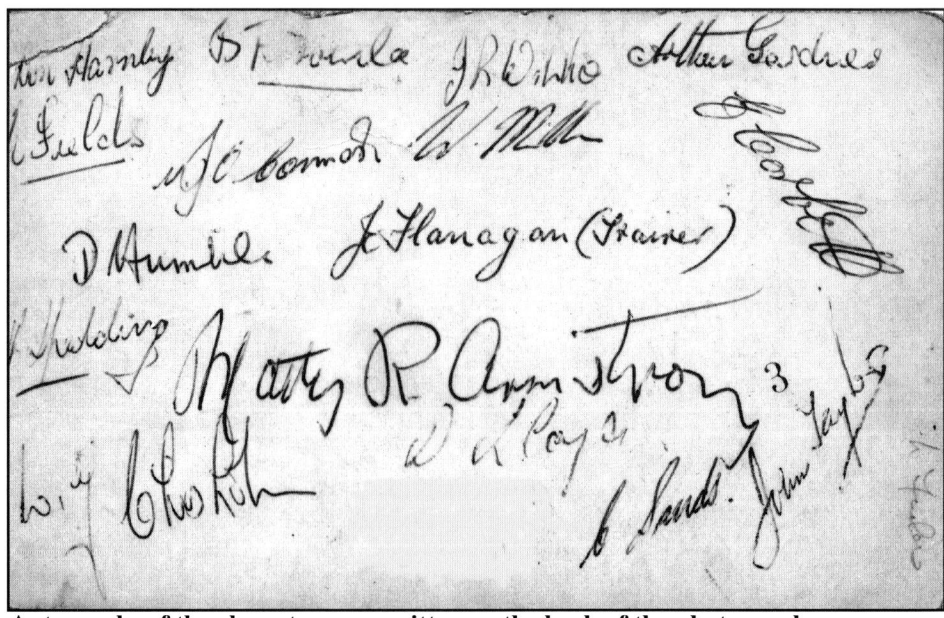

Autographs of the above team as written on the back of the photograph.

SPENNYMOOR REMEMBERED – BOOK 3

Cross Street Concert Party 1940.
Children of King William Street, King James street and Cross Street in Tudhoe Grange, who have been organising without adult assistance, backyard concerts to raise funds for the Red cross. Their ages range from two to fourteen, and they have been trained by Enid Redhead aged eleven and Beatrice Biddle aged thirteen. Natty Redhead, aged thirteen was producer. Accompaniment was provided by Cliff Nichols (drums) and Jack Nichols (piano accordion). Admission charges were a penny for adults and halfpenny for children. On this occasion £2 was raised. Children taking part were: Beatrice Biddle, Dolly Redhead, Enid Redhead, Natty Redhead, Cliff Nichols, Jacky Nichols, Hilda Perry, Doreen Sugden, Mary Savage, Doreen Rowntree, Betty Rowntree, Edith Woodlands, Lydia Young, June Ryder, Beatrice Ryder, Harry Ryder, Irene Brumwell and Audrey Groves.

Siemens Keep Fit Club Christmas Party 1948.

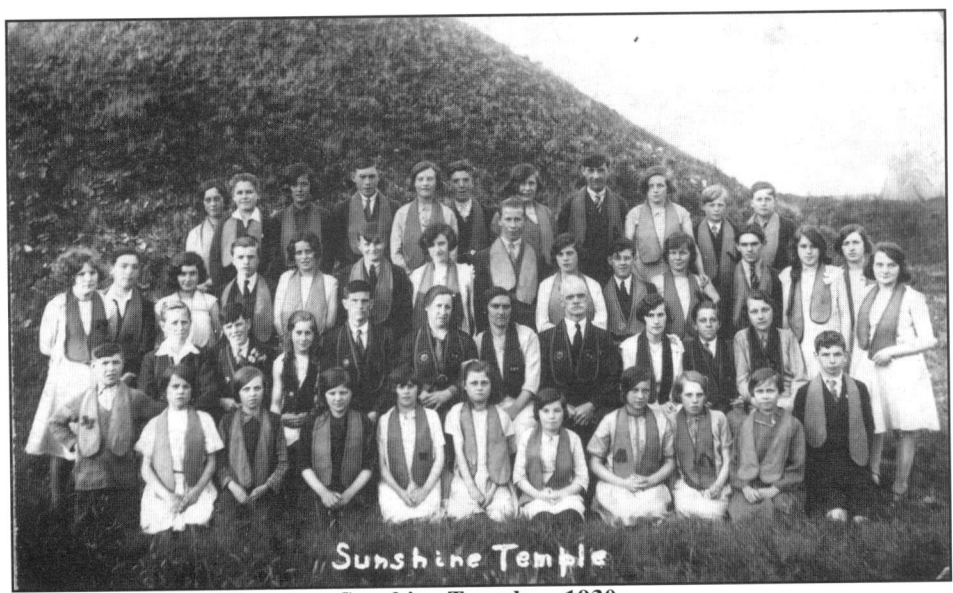

Spennymoor Good Templars Sunshine Temple c. 1930.
The Templars had a strong following in Spennymoor based at Templar Hall in Cheapside. There was also branches at Tudhoe Colliery and Low Spennymoor. This was the junior section of the Spennymoor branch the photograph being taken at the base of one of the slag heaps behind Templar Hall.

Tudhoe Colliery Carnival Float c. 1910
A wet day for the occasion, whatever it might have been. The children are on Tudhoe Co-op cart.

SPENNYMOOR REMEMBERED – BOOK 3

Zion Chapel Oxford Street c. 1950.

The Zion Chapel was built in 1859 for the Methodist New Connection congregation at the expense of Mr. Joseph Long. In 1874 it was greatly enlarged and a gallery added at the cost of £700, which included the purchase of the site and the organ. The new building was of stone, with a gabled frontage of white brick and could seat approximately 400. Over the years the congregation of the church dwindled until in the early 1920's it was so small that it met in a room at the back of the chapel rather than in the main building.

Spennymoor Assembly.

As a result of a campaign in the district by Stephen Jeffreys the Spennymoor Assemble was formed being a part of the Pentecostal Movement. Pastor Jim Techner was asked to take on the new work. The Methodist New Connection were asked if the Spennymoor Assembly could use the building on a Sunday night after their service had finished. This arrangement continued up until 1950 when they were able to buy the building from the Methodists. The chapel was renamed the Zion Pentecostal Church. The old Zion Chapel continued to be used up until it was demolished in 1965. The demolition came about because the Local Council wanted to construct a new road (Oxford Road) to carry traffic round behind the new shopping precinct and the chapel was an obstruction to that work. The Methodist chapel at the top of Weardale Street was offered as an alternative place of worship, however Pastor J. Meale objected strongly on the grounds that it was too far for his congregation to travel. He won the day and the new chapel was built on land adjacent to the Victoria Inn. The New chapel, The Assemblies of God was opened on 23rd. April 1966. These premises eventually became too small for the growing congregation and it was sold to become the present doctor's surgery. The present home of the congregation is in the premises, which were once the drill hall, situated in Villiers Street.

Zion Chapel Picnic c.1930.
The picnic was an annual event usually taking place near or in Middlestone Village. This is a photograph of one of the earliest ones.
Among others: Mrs. Johnson, Wilf Maughan and Mr. K. Rowlands.

List of Pastors officiating in the old chapel.
Jim Techener   1927 - 1930
Mrs. Techner   1930 - 1943
Osborne Smith   1943 - 1944 for three months
J. B. Pears   1944 - 1950
Jeffries Williamson   1950 - 1953
J. Scott   1953 - 1959
J. Meale   1959 - 1966

Pastors since the demolition of the old chapel.
Without a pastor for two years.
Pastor Morean   1971 for 10 months
Pastor J. Lease   1972 - 1976
Pastor Hiles   1976 - 1983
Pastor Webb   1983 for few months
David Mathews   1984 - 1985
Richard Gibson   1987

The above information was provided by Gilbert Anderson who was a member of the church from when it started in 1927. He eventually became Sunday School Superintendent in 1943 and served in this capacity for 31 years until 1974.

SPENNYMOOR REMEMBERED – BOOK 3

Interior of the Zion Chapel c. 1952.
The occasion being the celebration of the anniversary of Pastor Jeffery Williamsons coming to Spennymoor. His wife Nancy is about to cut the cake.

Local Pastors outside the Zion Chapel c. 1950.
Left to right:
Pastor Miss Nan Logan, West Auckland Pentecostal Church; Pastor Geoffrey Williamson, Spennymoor Zion Chapel; Pastor Raymond Potter, Ferryhill Assemblies of God; Pastor Norman Humphrey, Houghton le Spring Assemblies of God and Mr. Ted Coates, children's worker.

Zion Chapel c. 1948.
Among others: Mrs. Johnson, Dot Wilkinson, Miss Katy Cooper, Joyce Healey, Gilbert Anderson, Mrs. Gill, Mrs. Robinson, Pastor Jim Pears, Mrs. Lily Anderson, Mrs. Blackburn and Bill Healey.

Opening ceremony for the new Assemblies of God Church April 1966.

Middlestone Moor Basketball Team 1972.
Left to right Back Row: John Thorogood, H. Hodgson, John Gibbons, Ian Appleby, John Richardson, and Stewart Mitchell. Front Row: Bob Abley, Barry Winter, Alan Wilkinson, Anthony Forster, Billy Cooper and Glyn Williams.

The team was formed in 1970 and played in the Wearside League. They were based in Middlestone Moor Youth Club but as the playing facilities were below the league standard they later moved to Spennymoor West Modern School and became known as Spennymoor West old Boys.

Gala Day, July 1970. Waiting for the Parade.

Nutter's Buildings 1929.

Edward, Prince of Wales, at Nutter's Buildings in 1929 during his tour of North East mining communities. Seen above in the backyard of Bill Lindsay's house.

Spennymoor Cycle Track c.1905.
Four men and their machines said to be sat at the side of Spennymoor cycle track which was situated in the area known today as "the valley" between Ox Close Crescent and Deneside. The track was in the valley bottom and straddled the open beck, which ran through it at that time. The spectators sat on the Deneside slope to watch the races.

FIVE

TRADE AND INDUSTRY

Mobile crane at the Weardale Works c.1890.
 This splendid photograph and the two following were taken in the last decade of the working life of the Iron and Steel works. The works had opened in 1855 to produce pig iron from ore mined in Weardale and coke produced locally. The works closed in 1901 when the owners moved their steel making operation to Teeside, throwing hundreds of men and boys out of work. Local supplies of iron ore being exhausted brought about the move to Teeside, Teeside being better situated to receive supplies of imported iron ore. After the closure of the iron and steel works the site was used for the manufacture of coal by-products and finally ceased working altogether in 1955.

SPENNYMOOR REMEMBERED - BOOK 3

Blast Furnace Workers c.1895.
Despite the fact that the iron and steel works closed down in 1901 there were occasion when the furnaces were relit and production resumed. There were three occasions when this happened: 1906 for a very short period of time, for the duration of World War 1 and in 1926. After 1926 the furnaces were never used again.

Tudhoe Grange Colliery c. 1870

Two collieries were sunk by the Weardale Iron and Coal Company to provide coke and coal for the operation of the Iron and Steel Works. The first of these was Tudhoe Colliery begun in 1865 the first coals being drawn in November 1866. The other being Tudhoe Grange Colliery, the sinking, beginning on 5th.May 1869, the first coals being drawn on 23rd. of December 1870.

Tudhoe Grange Colliery was sunk in the triangle of land formed by the junction of Weardale Street with Coulson Street, see sketch map below below.

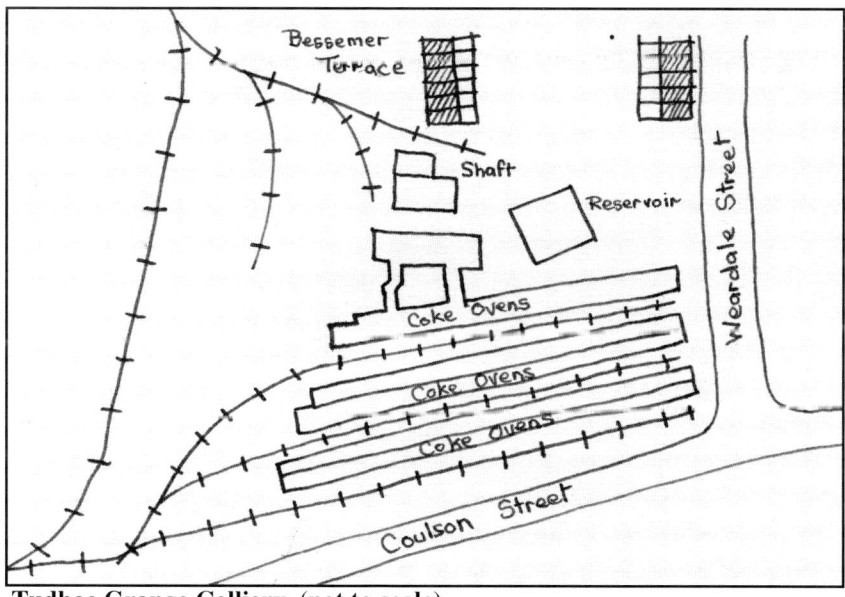

Tudhoe Grange Colliery. (not to scale)

SPENNYMOOR REMEMBERED - BOOK 3

By 1877 three seams were being worked at Tudhoe Grange; the Brockwell at a depth of 492ft, the Harvey at 378 feet and the Hutton at 288 feet. Due to the slackness of trade and the stocks of coke held at that time output had been restricted to 270 ton a day instead of the normal 370 tons a day. This reduced output meant that miners had to be laid off work. Conditions were so uncertain that the owners were looking into the feasibility of laying the pit in until trade improved. At this time the coke ovens and iron and steel works were consuming the following amounts of coal:

Coke Ovens   450 tons per week
Iron Works   600 tons per week
Mixing   80 to 100 tons per week (the mixing was done to improve the other works coal.)

Ten men worked in the Brockwell seam and there was very little coal left in it. The manager John Laverick calculated that the seam had a remaining life of 21 months. The Brockwell seam produced the best coking coal. It cost 4s. .. 2d. (approx. 21p.) to produce a ton of coal in this seam of which 1shilling (5p.) was paid to the coal hewer.

The Harvey seam was the seam that the whole future of the pit depended upon, it was reached by a drift from the Brockwell. The cost of making the drift had been in excess of £1,000. Twenty-four men were employed in this seam which varied in thickness from 28 inches to 34 inches. They were having difficulty in developing the seam because of geological problems, it was only producing 40 tons a day. They were only averaging four tubs of coal per man shift in this seam as opposed to the Brockwell, which averaged 10 tubs per man shift. It was anticipated that the seam would be producing 450 tons a day when the problems were sorted out.

The Hutton seam was producing 60 tons a day, which was half of the output that it had normally been producing some months previously. They had reached the boundary of the royalty where the seam had been at its thickest, they now had to revert to the narrower part of the seam making the coal harder to get and uneconomic. It cost nearly 6 shillings (approx.. 30p.) to produce a ton of coal in this seam.

The colliery closed down when the iron works closed in 1901, however it is possible that production in the colliery had halted long before then, the shaft up to its closure being used to draw up coals from Tudhoe Colliery.

North Close Colliery.

This colliery was also known as Merrington Park Colliery and was also nicknamed the Rock Pit. The site of this pit is on the land in Rock Road that was used by J. E. Key and Sons as a coal depot. There were four shafts and a drift mouth on the site. It is not certain when the pit was first sunk but it is thought to have been in the 1880's, the first sinking being made to the Busty of Five-Quarter seam. This seam was worked out by about 1915 and in 1916 a shaft was sunk to the Main Coal or the Hutton seam. The Hutton was worked up until 1921 when a shaft was sunk into the Low main or the Durham Low Main seam. This seam was worked until the closure of the pit in 1927. The name change from North Close Colliery to Merrington Colliery came about around

1910, the reason not being known, it could have been due to the abandoning of the Busty seam and working the higher seams.

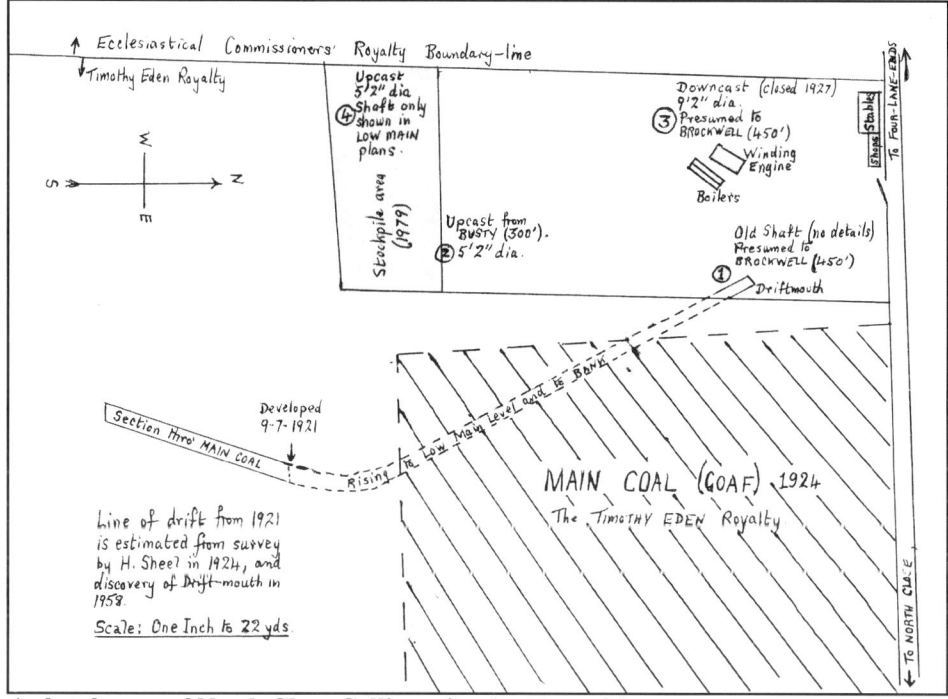

A sketch map of North Close Colliery site. (not to scale)

Around 1920 a drift to the Main coal was driven to bank, it is possible that it was originally a staple connecting the Main coal with the Low Main coal and was driven to bank as the original shafts were no longer safe. The pit closed on 8th. August 1927 and the drift renamed Rock drift was taken over by Binchester Colliery. The drift was used as a travelling way for Binchester workman and as a "nip out" a means of escape in case of an accident for Binchester Colliery.

The pit seems to have been owned for a good part of its working life by the Olivers' father and son from Merrington. The father Robert Oliver lived in Prospect House in Merrington and owned a tailor's shop (see page 124) he also had a branch in Clyde Terrace in Spennymoor. They were also part owners of Whitworth Colliery at one time, after the closure of the pit in 1927 the son also Robert became a farmer in Merrington.

The late Jack Gillan, the well-known bookmaker, worked in the pit from time to time up to the 1920's. Jack always had a picturesque turn of phrase below are some of the recollections of his time there:

"The pit was run and worked by bookie's runners, musicians and broken down landlords." It is not known who was which or what, but it has been established that the reference to "musicians" appertained to Inky Heseltine who played the bass fiddle in the Cambridge theatre orchestra. Inky used to say that, "Nee matter what happens to the pit, I have a big fiddle that'll keep me."

SPENNYMOOR REMEMBERED - BOOK 3

Herbert Robson was overman; George Gray the deputy and a chap called Tindale was banksman. In Jack Gillans words, "The pit was nowt more than a "blacking" factory and run on temporary labour, Yer never knew who was goin' to turn up for work or when." The term blacking factory implies that the amount of coals produced was just enough to make a few tins of boot blacking.

In 1983 a liscense was granted for a drift to be driven into the Hutton seam at Middlestone Moor, it was intended to give employment to 20 men and to produce 50,000 tons of coal over an eight-year period. This was the Lonnen Drift near Nannypop Lonnen.

Lonnen Drift mouth c.1985

Middlestone Moor Drift (the Dickie Pit)

The nickname of "Dickie Pit" was applied to all small landsale pits. There were two shafts and a drift all in the Shafto Royalty.

The Number 1 shaft was sunk c.1850 to the Low main seam at about 50 feet, a drift then went from the shaft bottom in a northerly direction towards Whitworth Park Colliery Main Coal seam, and holed through approximately in the area of Whitworth Lane. (Marked no.1 on map on page 109)

The Number 2 shaft was sunk c. 1926 to the Hutton at 120 feet and acted as an air shaft. (marked no.2 on the map)

The Drift was driven upwards from the Hutton seam towards the Four Lane Ends area, and drew coals from 1936 until 1960.

SPENNYMOOR REMEMBERED - BOOK 3

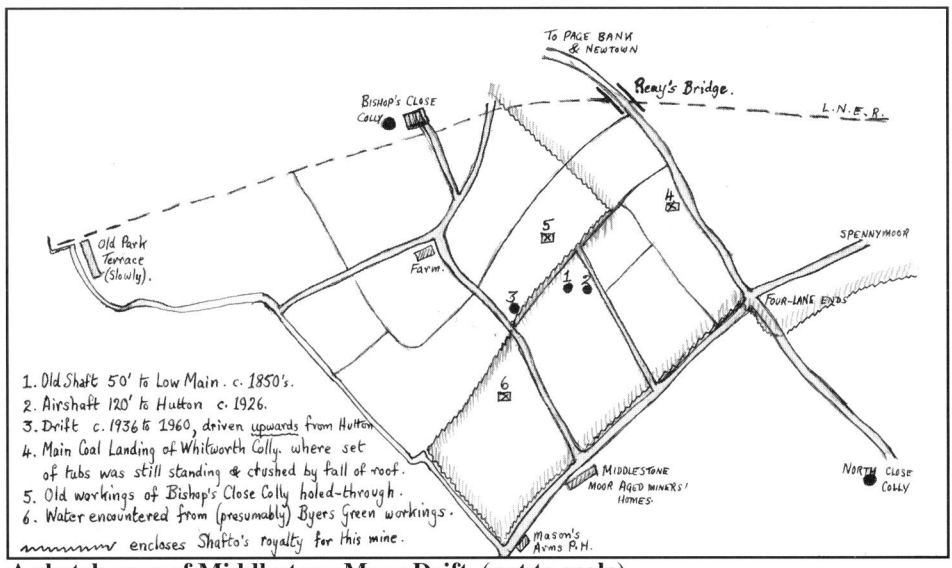

A sketch map of Middlestone Moor Drift. (not to scale)

Prior to 1936 the pit was owned by William Elwood, of Oak Terrace Spennymoor, and his brother in law. Edward Lowe was manager of the pit several years before and up to 1935. He operated the pit with 20 men, which was the maximum he could employ with an undermanager. If there had been no undermanager he would only have been able to employ 9 men. Among the men working at the pit were:
Jimmy Hunter of Middlestone Moor
Stan Hunter of Spennymoor
Rueben Kellet of Bishop Auckland
Billy Spowart of Chestnut Avenue
Tommy Spowart, father of the above
"Arrd" Clayton of Edward Street Spennymoor
Joe Ogilvey of Albion Street
Joe Stone Bank of Albion Street Middlestone moor
Thomas Holmes who was the cutterman
Jim Milburn who was the haulerman
Geordie Ridley
Joe Hattley
Archie Knight
Cecil Knight
Jimmy Bolam
"Nobbler" Knowles
Eddie Trotter
Bob Minto.

The cutter was an electric Sisskel & Hardy machine and Tommy Holmes worked it. It was a dual-purpose machine, which could be used to power a drill. The drill often broke down and the holes had to be drilled by the monkey and worm method (by hand). This early type of cutter was an arc-wall type machine i.e. it was set in a stationary position and swung around from left to right on its base plate, the pick arm or jib making jabs at the coal face, hence the name "punch" cutter. The machine was winched under its own power by rope drum, chain and station, to its next arc position along the face.

The shaft winder was steam powered by a vertical cylinder and the same steam turbine generated the electricity, which drove the main and tail hauler at the foot of the shaft. When the drift came into coal drawing it was used all the way to bank, it only pulled four tubs at a time, each tub being of 6cwt. Capacity, up the drift on main-rope only and only employed the tail rope when hauling to and from the landing at the bottom of the drift. Eddie Trotter was a putter in 1936 and said that there were non back-ower turns, or swapes (sweeps) to negotiate. It was all straight rails with flatsheets laid at every turn. No ponies were ever used in the pit.

Water troubles were encountered in the "dickie" pit at shaft number 2 when they approached the old workings of Byers Green colliery.they had no pumping system and the only managed to keep going by siphoning water off into the old workings of Whitworth Colliery Main Coal seam.

The main engine plane, in the pit, ran from the "dickie"pit to the Main Coal seam at Whitworth Colliery. On holing through, the engine plane was found to have been closed up at one point by a heavy fall, and tubs were standing in the landing as when the work had finished. No attempt had been made to salvage anything. To reach Whitworth Colliery Main Seam from the "dickie" pit side, Edward Lowe said that he had to pass under the area of a collapsed old shaft. The cages were at the bottom of the shaft holding up all the collapsed stone and rubble. He had to walk through the cage to get to the other side of the waggonway and workings.

The old number 1 shaft collapsed in 1960 through lack of maintenance. There was no one in the pit at the time, the cage fell to the bottom of the shaft and the pit was closed. Everything was left there as it was at the time of the collapse.

Whitworth Colliery.

Whitwoth Park Colliery was the foundation on which Spennymoor was built. With the establishing of the colliery between 1836 and 1841 there was an influx of miners and their families into the area. Housing was needed for them and so the cluster of cottages built adjacent to the pit formed the embryo of Spennymoor, as we know it today. Even from its earliest days the pit had a chequered career, no sooner had the first coals been drawn from the pit the owning company, the Durham County Coal Company went bankrupt. Shortly after it was taken over by another company and another shaft was sunk and was called Merrington Colliery. The pit did not really thrive until it came into the hands of Thomas Reay during the 1860's and 1870's. Reay made a good deal of money from the pit and became one of the prominent members of the community. It is said that in one year he made £80,000 profit, which in those days was a small fortune. Out of the wealth created by the pit he built Whitworth House, however, he lost the fortune that he had made by investing it in an unsuccessful pit in another area. The railway bridge taking Whitworth Lane over the railway was called Reay's Bridge after him. The pit closed in 1883 as a result of the great world recession at the time. Other attempts were made to operate the pit and the only really successful one was when it was reopened in 1945 after the Second world war when coal supplies were short.

Whitworth Park Colliery 1952

Whitworth Park Colliery 1969

Whitworth Pit being demolished 1975.
The pit eventually closed on 2nd June 1974.

I started work at Whitworth Pit in 1945 aged 15 years, I had already been working at Mainsforth Pit for a year after leaving school. I started work on bank and graduated through various jobs until I was coal hewing. I did hand putting, as there were no horses at Whitworth, I also did stone work and drilling. It was hard work and the conditions weren't very good, the seams were low, about 18inches and it was wet, as there were no pumps. The seams were so narrow that if you went in with your shovel the wrong way round you had to back out to put it the right way round. It was so narrow in places that at the end of the shift you came out skinned. Things improved a bit after Nationalisation in 1947 when we got pumps to take the water away and eventually we got baths.

Overall I worked 21 years at Whitworth and during that time three men were killed, two by falls of stone and one crushed by a skip, there were men always getting injured. In 1954 I got married and was then being paid about £8 per week. We bought a one bedroomed house over in William Street in Low Spennymoor for £200, I thought we would never pay it off. Most of my family were miners or connected with mining. My Dad's father was a blacksmith in Merrington Lane, he was a Quaker and originally from Darlington. My mother's father brought his family up from Staffordshire to work in the pits. He had been a "legger" on barges on the canals, he used to lie in top of the barge and use his legs to push the barges through tunnels.

I left Whitworth Pit and started work at Courtauld's who had just opened up their factory in Spennymoor. I made the move because I had hurt my back and was finding it difficult to work at the pit. Courtauld's closed down and I finished the rest of my working life at Tomados

Bob Richmond.

SPENNYMOOR REMEMBERED - BOOK 3

I worked at Mainsforth Pit for a year, Billy Griffith and me were seconded from Mainsforth Pit in 1956 to help introduce power loading at Whitorth. We were employed as cuttermen for the power loader it wasn't a success but we stopped there for a year. The manager was Patterson, he was also the manager of Tudhoe Colliery. The under manager was Tommy Murray who we ended up working for on composite work, that is we were employed on any work that he thought fit to give us. We were paid £16 .. 10shillings a week and worked mainly day shift, our starting time varied according to the job we were doing. We didn't have to join Whitworth Union Lodge but had to contribute towards the pension fund at 1shilling and 6 pence a week, which translates to about £3 on the pension that I get now.

Whitworth was one of the lowest pits in the county, the seams varied between 15 and 18 inches. You had a small shovel and a crackett to rest your shoulder on while hewing coal. Safety regulations weren't all that the might be and it was a hard pit but it was a good pit to work in it was a family pit everybody knew everybody else.

Whitworth was one of the only pits in the county who took on refugees from Hungary, after the rising. I remember six of them coming to do six months training while I was there. They were given an instructor each who showed them the ropes, how to do the job, how to draw their pay etc. At bait time they always had cheese, raw onion and bread. At the end of the six months they all disappeared.

Michael Bostock (senior)

Whitworth Colliery c. 1965.

Whitworth Park Coal Company.

From 1883 no work was done at Whitworth Colliery until 1926 when the Whitworth Park Coal Company. put down a drift called the Page Bank drift to work the Harvey Seam. The first coals were drawn on Christmas Eve 1929. The first sod was broken by

SPENNYMOOR REMEMBERED - BOOK 3

Bert Rawe a Cockfield man. Bert travelled from Cockfield for five months before getting a house in Byers Green. Other miners who helped drive the shaft were Harry Wilkinson, Joe Stevens, George Nicholson and Jack Bowden, they were all Cockfield men. Later other families moved from Cockfield to Byers Green to work the drift including the Thompsons, Gilbert and Maurice Shaw, Cecil Chapman and Teddy Bowes. Bert Rawe was a shareholder in the consortium with Jack Simpson, Summerson and Brydon.

During the 1930's an aerial flight was bought from either Pelton Fell or Waldridge Collieries for £60. Apparently the sellers threw in some tubs and other pit gear for good measure. The aerial flight was used to transport the coal from the drift up the hill to the Merrington Colliery site where it was washed, screened and stocked in a coal depot there for landsale.

The drift closed when the Merrington Colliery site reopened in 1945 as Whitworth Park Colliery, all coals from that time were wound up the Merrington Colliery Shaft. The NCB took over Whitworth park colliery on vesting day in 1947 the seams worked were the Hutton, Harvey, Top Busty and Brockwell

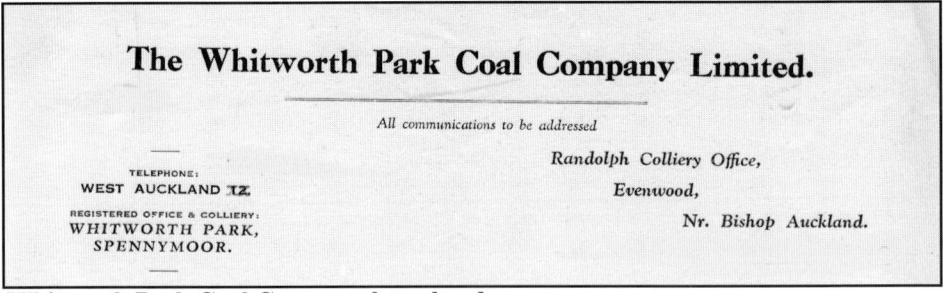

The Whitworth Park Coal Company Limited.

All communications to be addressed

TELEPHONE:
WEST AUCKLAND 12.

REGISTERED OFFICE & COLLIERY:
WHITWORTH PARK,
SPENNYMOOR.

Randolph Colliery Office,
Evenwood,
Nr. Bishop Auckland.

Whitworth Park Coal Company letterhead.

Whitworth Park Colliery 1955.

There were two seams worked in 1955, the Harvey and the Top Busty. The coal thickness if the Harvey Seam is 1 foot 10inches and the Busty Seam is 1 foot 9 inches.
In 1955 83,507 tons of coal were raised and weighed from the pit.
The average daily output was 330tons of which 235 tons were Harvey and 95 tons Busty. A boring programme was carried out in 1955 and the Top Busty coal was found to be a good workable proposition.
The resources at Whitworth Park colliery warrant a future working life for the colliery of 43 years, based on current output.
The number of men employed at Whitworth Park Colliery is 295 of which 230 are employed underground and 65 on the surface.

Margaret Pit, Whitworth.

This was the third working shaft to be sunk at Whitworth, it was sunk sometime after the other shafts and was worked up until 1883. It had a one-tub cage and rode two men according to the late John Cornish it also had ladders and platforms. Apparently miners used to use this shaft as a shortcut to their workplace if ever they were late for work. There were no token checks in those days and men had their own lamps with them. Michael Bostock (senior) can remember playing in this shaft as a child, during the

SPENNYMOOR REMEMBERED - BOOK 3

1940's and getting right to the shaft bottom and into the pit through big wooden doors. Michael can remember that there was a strong draught coming up the shaft from the pit.

I left school North Road School on the Friday night and went to Dean and Chapter on the Monday morning to get a job. I went in my best clothes thinking I would have an interview and then come home. The bloke I saw said,"screens." and that's where I ended up that day, picking stones out of the coal on the screens in my best clothes. I can remember walking down the pit road after I had finished the shift and I was absolutely filthy. After I worked on the screens for a while I did my sixteen weeks training at Dean and Chapter. When the training was complete I went underground and worked as a tippler in the Harvey seam. This was in 1949 and my first pay packet was 30 shillings (£1.50). From Dean and Chapter I moved to Bowburn for a while and in 1954 at the age of 19 I started work at Whitworth and I was there for twenty years until it closed. At Whitworth I did datal work and the on-setting (drawing coal). My marrers were Harry Mathews and Doug Raine, Doug played football for West Auckland. Whitworth was a family pit, everybody knew everybody else, most of the men were from Spennymoor, Byers Green and Page Bank. By the time I was married in 1957 I was earning £11 a week. There were two seams worked in the pit the Busty and the Harvey both of them narrow. We worked three shifts, nightshift (12 midnight), dayshift (8 on a morning) and back shift (4 on an afternoon) and were usually in the pit for seven and a half-hours

E. Hodges

The last ponies out of Metal Bridge Drift

Dean and Chapter Colliery.
From left to right: J.Stevenson, G.Toas, R. Northcote and Sam Hamilton working water drilling machines at Dean and Chapter c.1947.

Binchester Colliery Pit Head Gear.
 This photograph was taken prior to demolition in 1962. The site was being used as Westerton Drift at this time.

SPENNYMOOR REMEMBERED - BOOK 3

Westerton Drift c.1960.

Tudhoe Park Drift c.1950.
Tudhoe Park Drift opened in 1941 and ceased production in 1968. The high building in the background is the screens, the drift mouth is on the extreme right. At the front left is the joiner's and blacksmith's shop.

Tudhoe Colliery Workmen c.1935
George Brumwell is second from the left holding a shovel.

Mainsforth Colliery 1923.
The colliery was owned by Dorman, Long and Company at this time. Mainsforth was a source of employment for Spennymoor miners for a good number of years.

SPENNYMOOR REMEMBERED - BOOK 3

Spennymoor Goods Station Staff c. 1930.
Left to right: Sheila Dodshon, Alice Loverton, and Marjorie Mattison.

Spennymoor Goods station Staff c.1930
Left to right: Norman Hind (goods porter), Ivy King (clerk), engine driver, Miss Carr, (clerk) and engine driver.

SPENNYMOOR REMEMBERED - BOOK 3

Spennymoor Goods Station Staff c. 1930.
Among others: Charlie Jackson, Betty Richards, Bob Guy, Miss Carr and Norman Hind.

Spennymoor Goods Station Staff c. 1930.
Among others: Sheila Dodshon, Alice Loughton

SPENNYMOOR REMEMBERED - BOOK 3

Spennymoor Station Master c.1950.
Mr. Arthur Stabler with his daughter Phoebe who worked as a clerk at the station.

BRITISH RAILWAYS

TRAIN SERVICE

FERRYHILL and SPENNYMOOR

27th SEPTEMBER 1948 until further notice

Table 60							B					
		am	am	am	pm	pm	pm					
FERRYHILL .... dep		8 20	9 30	10 45	4 26	6 45	8 42	....	....	...	...	...
SPENNYMOOR .... arr		8 30	9 40	10 55	4 36	6 55	8 52	...	...	...	...	...

WEEKDAYS (One Class only)

			C			A						
		am	am	am	am	pm	pm					
SPENNYMOOR .... dep		7 30	10 0	10 20	11 15	4 55	7 20	....	....	....	....	....
FERRYHILL .... arr		7 38	10 8	10 28	11 23	5 3	7 28	...	...	...	...	...

A—Through Train to Stockton arrive 5-36 pm   B—Through Train from Darlington depart 8-20 pm
C—Through Train to Darlington arrive 10-30 am

SPENNYMOOR REMEMBERED - BOOK 3

Prospect House, Kirk Merrington c.1900.
The residence and business premises of Robert Oliver tailor, draper and colliery owner. Later had a shop in Clyde Terrace, Spennymoor.

Henderson's Shop, Middlestone Moor c, 1900

SPENNYMOOR REMEMBERED - BOOK 3

Henderson Family c.1890

Timothy with wife Emma (Nee Bolton) and their sons George and Alfred. Timothy and his family owned and ran a general dealers shop in Middlestone Moor up until about 1920. Timothy's father had been a farmer in the area possibly farming the land that is Jewitt's farm at the present time. He also had a shop at Ferryhill at Bridge End. Alfred moved to West Auckland and opened a shop there, George moved down south and opened a retail business.

George Henderson with Ford Delivery Van c.1910.

SPENNYMOOR REMEMBERED - BOOK 3

This was one of the first ford delivery vans to be used in the Spennymoor area.

Vincent's Coach c. 1930

    The coach and horses belonged to Fred Vincent of Attwood Terrace, Tudhoe Colliery, his son John is driving. The Vincent brothers John and Billy came to Croxdale from Cornwall in the 1880's to work in the colliery there, they didn't like the work and took to farming, carting and operating horse busses. They were one of the first to start a horse drawn bus service in the area. Their first service was transporting nuns from Salvin's Hall in Croxdale up to Tudhoe Homes.

    In the 1890's the Vincents moved up to Attwood Terrace, living next door to each other and from here worked as miners and brake proprietors, and by 1905 had acquired their first motorised double decker bus. John Vincent died in 1925 and the business was taken over by his son Fred. Their premises consisted of stables and a tack room and there was a cesspool, the stables became a regular meeting place for locals who wanted to gossip.

    They owned the field opposite Tudhoe Colliery School for grazing their horses and had some land up by Gypsy Lonnen, which they farmed.

    Fred Vincent died in 1945, he died eating a rabbit pie, after his death the land and horses were sold off and that ended the connection with farming.

    Their premises were next to the picture house in Tudhoe Colliery, the Tudhoe Picture Palace.

Vincent's Hearse c.1915
In the driving seat is old John Vincent ands in the background the stables and tackroom

Domenic's Ice Cream Cart c.1920.
The photograph was taken at the bottom end of Marmaduke Street looking along Low Grange Road.

SPENNYMOOR REMEMBERED - BOOK 3

Muttons Boot and Shoe Works c. 1910.

George Mutton started his boot and shoe making business in Tudhoe Colliery in 1903. He was deaf and dumb and had attended the Royal School for the Deaf in Newcastle where he had learned his trade. He gradually learned to talk when his wife and him had a family, there were four boys and the need to communicate with them gave him the incentive and encouragement he needed., Although times were hard during the 1920's his business did quite well in comparison to others. Although there were no social services there was a boot fund to provide boots and their repair for children who were in need and it was from this trade that he kept going. He retired from the business in 1953 and it was taken over by his son Bill.

Bill had been trained in the business by his father, as he was the oldest of the four boys. He worked for a while for his keep for his father but because he wouldn't pay a wage he left to work at Hood's the Cobblers in Spennymoor. As a result of a recruiting campaign in 1938, he joined the Territorial Army along with Johnny and Fred Hood to get the bounty that was offered. When war was declared in 1939 they were among the first lot to be sent abroad. Johnny Hood and Bill were together for the duration of the war in North Africa and when demobbed both went back to work in the Hood's business. Bill worked for the Hood's until he took over his fathers business in 1953.

During the 1960' when the Middle and Back Rows were demolished in Tudhoe Colliery he lost a lot of business as most of the population moved away to Middlestone Moor. A relative at Middlesone Moor took orders in for him and a shop in Durham did the same and despite the difficulties he kept going until the early 1970's when he took the caretakers job at Tudhoe Colliery School. This was ideal as he worked split shifts, which enabled him to still do some cobbling. He worked for 12 years at the school before he had to retire.

SPENNYMOOR REMEMBERED - BOOK 3

Bill Mutton.
In his workshop on the occasion of his retirement.

William's Chip Van. The first chip van in Spennymoor, sited outside the Commercial Hotel from 1908 until 1936. William Henry Williams is working the van.

SPENNYMOOR REMEMBERED - BOOK 3

Remains of the Detonator Factory in Middlestone Moor 1973.

Between 1918 and 1920 Noble's Explosives Ltd., a founder company of I.C.I. built a factory for the manufacture of detonators for the local pits. The factory was built in an isolated position beside the Westerton, Ferryhill Colliery Line to the south of Middlestone Moor. Shortly after it opened, there was an explosion said to be caused by a man carrying too many boxes of detonators, he managed to drop one and in the resulting explosion he was literally blown to pieces, not a shred of his body or clothing were recovered. Some of the girls who worked in the factory were also injured.

At the time of the explosion Noble's Ltd. were building another factory in Ayr, in Scotland and rather than reopen the Middlestone Moor factory they moved the production to Ayr. The factory was let go to ruin and around 1970 the buildings were demolished leaving the foundations as shown above in the photograph.